HATCH PEPPER
COOKBOOK

Sharon Hernandez, Chef Ida Rodriguez, & Chef Tom Fraker

Published in the United States by World Variety Produce, Inc.

Library of Congress Control Number: 2021936897

ISBN-13: 978-0-9906443-4-7
UPC: 0 45255-15350 7

Distributed by:
World Variety Produce, Inc.
PO Box 514599
Los Angeles, CA 90051

To order, contact Melissa's:
800-588-0151
www.melissas.com
hotline@melissas.com

Photography:
Melissa's/World Variety
Produce, Inc.

Printed in Canada
10 9 8 7 6 5 4 3 2 1

HATCH
PEPPER
COOKBOOK

Melissa's/World Variety Produce, Inc., is known for the freshest ideas in produce. Company founders Sharon and Joe Hernandez, along with their daughter, Melissa, have introduced exotic, conventional, and organic produce items to Food Lovers across the nation.

Melissa's/World Variety Produce leads the industry in supplying delicious and delectable-tasting fruits and vegetables to supermarkets and venues all over the world. In the professional culinary world, Melissa's has long been recognized as an extraordinary supplier for the freshest and tastiest fruits and vegetables. World-renowned chefs insist upon Melissa's Produce for their signature restaurants.

Melissa's consistently shares what's in season with you, to bring the flavors of the world to your kitchen. Please visit us at www.melissas.com and be sure to look and ask for Melissa's brand in your local produce department.

Table *of* Contents

HATCH PEPPER

Introduction

It's a long-standing tradition for our Melissa's family to end every summer with Hatch Peppers. Harvested from fertile soil along the Rio Grande, these prized Hatch Peppers are grown in Hatch, New Mexico. Rows and rows of mild, medium, hot, and extra hot peppers thrive in the river valley. Unlike any other pepper-growing region, Hatch's combination of nutrient-rich soil, intense sunlight, and cool desert nights results in this sought-after pepper with thick walls and meaty, flavorful flesh unlike any other.

Melissa's Hatch Peppers are the perfect addition to recipes to add mild to hot heat, as well as a flavor distinct to this pepper. During Hatch season, the spicy scent of peppers fills the air with food memories that tease our taste buds of what's to come. Hatch Peppers are versatile and can be used in place of any peppers in your recipes. We use them in smoothies, desserts, casseroles, soups, salads—the list goes on.

Hatch Peppers are harvested within a short six-week season. Melissa's delivers these full-flavored peppers to your local supermarket, who may be able to roast them for you, or you can take them home and roast them yourself. Once you have your roasted peppers, add them to your favorite recipe or freeze them so you have them anytime you need until next year's harvest.

Fresh and roasted Hatch Peppers aren't the only way enjoy this delicious pepper. We have created a Hatch Essential line to get your Hatch fix year-round: Hatch Clean Snax®, dried Hatch Pepper pods, Hatch pecans, Hatch popcorn, Hatch polenta, Hatch salsa, Hatch seasoning powder, and more.

Hatch, New Mexico

This coveted collection of Hatch recipes comes from our Melissa's family: Chef Tom Fraker, Chef Ida Rodriguez, Chef Raquel Perez, Chef Marco Zapien, and Chef Maggie Sajak. A special thanks to Robert Schueller, Melissa's Produce Guru, and to Melissa, herself.

All of these recipes are user friendly and palate pleasing, from the novice cook to sophisticated chef.

Happy Cooking®!

Sharon and Joe Hernandez
Founders and Owners

ESSENTIALS

HEAT LEVELS

Hatch Pepper varieties cover a full spectrum of heat levels: mild, medium, hot, and all the way to extra hot. They can be used interchangeably in all of our Hatch recipes. In the Mesilla Valley, pepper heat levels vary depending on the weather. Definitely do a pepper taste-test before adding to recipes to make sure your dish has just the right amount of heat.

STEP 1: ROASTING THE PEPPERS

Grilling: Our family thinks this is the best way to roast at home! Simply heat the grill, then line with peppers. Let your senses guide you to roasted perfection, giving them a quarter turn every few minutes and char them until the outer skin starts to blister and blacken.

Stovetop: Use long-handled metal tongs to hold the pepper over a medium open flame, turning often until evenly charred and the outer skin starts to blister and blacken.

Oven: Preheat broiler to high. Arrange peppers in a single layer on a baking sheet and set directly under the broiler. Roast until blackened and blistered all over, turning often.

Easiest way: Some local markets offer Melissa's Hatch Pepper roastings. All you need to do is show up and buy your peppers! Check out our website during Hatch season to see if there is a Melissa's roast near you! www.melissas.com

STEP 2: STEAMING THE PEPPERS

Once you've roasted your peppers, you'll want to let them steam in a closed container until cool to the touch before peeling. You can use a paper bag, a sheet pan covered with foil, or a bowl covered with a damp towel or plastic wrap over the top to get the job done.

STEP 3: PEELING THE PEPPERS

We recommend wearing disposable gloves when handling any pepper.
Once the peppers are cool to the touch, peel and discard skins,
revealing the silky flesh.

STEP 4: STORING & FREEZING

Once peeled, store in an airtight container in your refrigerator for 5-7 days.

Roasted Hatch Peppers can be frozen for up to 2 years. When frozen, Hatch Peppers become hotter over time. We recommend storing small portions to be used in recipes throughout the year.

Happy Roasting,

Chef Ida & Sharon

APPETIZERS

Sriracha and Hatch Pepper–Sauced Wings

Sriracha & Hatch Pepper–Sauced Wings

makes 4 to 6 servings

RUB

6 tablespoons smoked paprika

3 tablespoons garlic powder

2 tablespoons onion powder

1 tablespoon kosher salt

1 tablespoon freshly ground pepper

WINGS

3 pounds chicken wings

1 cup honey barbecue sauce

2 tablespoons sriracha

2 Melissa's Hatch Peppers, roasted, peeled, stemmed, seeded, and diced *(see Hatch Pepper Essentials, page 12)*

2 limes

For the rub, combine all of the rub ingredients in a large bowl. The rub may be stored in a tightly sealed container for up to 6 months if fresh ingredients are used.

Preheat the oven to 350°F. Grease a large baking sheet.

For the wings, add the wings to the rub, toss the wings, and rub evenly with the seasonings. Place the wings in a single layer on the baking sheet and bake for 30 minutes.

In a large bowl, combine the barbecue sauce, sriracha, and Hatch Peppers and mix well. Transfer the wings to the bowl and toss with the sauce to coat. Using a slotted spoon and reserving the remaining sauce, return the wings to the baking sheet and bake for 10 minutes. Transfer the wings to the bowl and toss to coat with the reserved sauce. Return the wings to the baking sheet and bake for an additional 10 minutes.

Remove the wings from the oven. Top the wings with the zest of the limes, squeeze the lime juice over them, and serve.

Turmeric Chicken Bites

makes 4 to 6 servings

MARINADE

½ cup Greek yogurt

Juice of 1 lime

4 cloves Melissa's Peeled Garlic, minced

1 tablespoon peeled minced fresh turmeric

1 tablespoon garam masala

2 teaspoons Melissa's Ground Ginger

¼ teaspoon Melissa's Hatch Pepper Powder, mild or hot

¼ teaspoon smoked paprika

1 pinch granulated sugar

Kosher salt and freshly ground pepper to taste

BITES

2 pounds boneless, skinless chicken breasts or thighs, cut into bite-size piece

Cooking spray

DIPPING SAUCE

1 cup Greek yogurt

Juice of 1 lime

1 teaspoon garlic salt

½ teaspoon Melissa's Hatch Pepper Powder, mild or hot

For the marinade, combine all of the marinade ingredients in a mixing bowl and mix well.

For the bites, add the chicken to the marinade and toss to coat well. Cover and place in the refrigerator for 6 to 7 hours.

Remove the chicken from the refrigerator and bring to room temperature. Preheat the oven to 350°F. Spray a baking sheet with cooking spray.

Place the chicken in a single layer on the baking sheet and bake for 12 to 15 minutes, or until the chicken reaches an internal temperature of 165°F, turning the chicken halfway through the cooking time.

For the dipping sauce, combine all of the dipping sauce ingredients in a small bowl and mix well. Serve with the hot chicken.

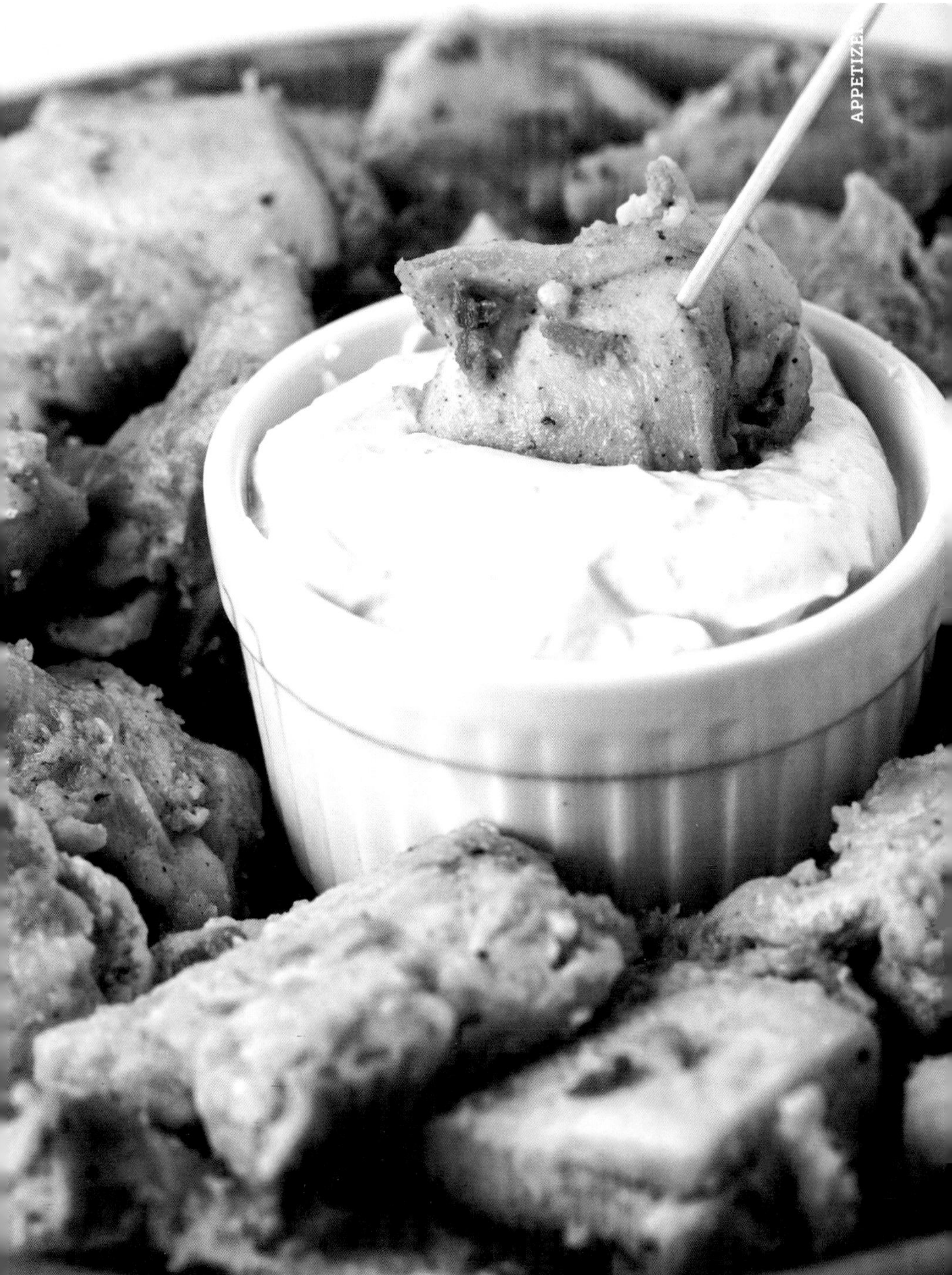

Crab & Veggie Sweet Pepper Endive Canapés *with* Tomatillo-Hatch Pepper Salsa

makes about 30 canapés and 1¹/₂ cups salsa

SALSA

5 Melissa's Fresh Tomatillos (about 10 ounces)

¼ Melissa's Perfect Sweet Onion, peeled

2 cloves Melissa's Peeled Garlic

½ teaspoon dried coriander

½ teaspoon dried oregano

¼ teaspoon ground cumin

2 tablespoons water

1 Melissa's Hatch Pepper, roasted, peeled, stemmed, and seeded
(see Hatch Pepper Essentials, page 12)

CANAPÉS

½ pound crabmeat

½ Roma tomato, finely diced

½ carrot, shredded

½ pound Melissa's Veggie Sweet Mini Peppers (about 10), stemmed, seeded, and finely diced

2 tablespoons fresh lime juice

3 tablespoons seasoned rice vinegar

Sea salt and freshly ground pepper

3 heads Belgium endive, ends trimmed and leaves separated

For the salsa, preheat the oven to 425°F.

Remove the thin husks from the tomatillos. Rinse the tomatillos and place them with the onion and garlic on a baking sheet. Place on the center rack of the oven and roast until they are moderately charred, about 15 minutes.

Once roasted, process the tomatillo mixture with the coriander, oregano, cumin, water, and Hatch Peppers to the desired texture in a blender.

For the canapés, pick through the crabmeat and discard any shell fragments. In a mixing bowl, combine the crabmeat, tomato, carrot, sweet peppers, lime juice, vinegar, and salt and pepper to taste and stir gently to mix. Cover and chill for up to 2 hours, or until ready to assemble.

To assemble, place a spoonful of the crab mixture on each endive leaf and top with a spoonful of salsa.

Crab & Hatch Pepper Cream Puffs

makes 14 to 16 filled cream puffs

PUFFS

1 quart water

10½ ounces (21 tablespoons) unsalted butter

2 tablespoons sugar

1 tablespoon (about) kosher salt

2 cups plus 2 tablespoons bread flour

12 large eggs

FILLING

1 pound lump crabmeat

8 ounces cream cheese, softened

8 hard-boiled eggs, chopped

½ cup mayonnaise

2 tablespoons Dijon mustard

½ Melissa's Perfect Sweet Onion, finely diced (about ½ cup)

2 ribs celery, finely diced

4 Melissa's Hatch Peppers, roasted, peeled, stemmed, seeded, and finely diced *(see Hatch Pepper Essentials, page 12)*

½ bunch Melissa's Fresh Cilantro, minced

Juice of 1 lime

¼ teaspoon Melissa's Red Hatch Pepper Powder, mild or hot

¼ teaspoon kosher salt

¼ teaspoon freshly ground pepper

For the puffs, preheat the oven to 450°F. Line a baking sheet with parchment paper.

Bring the water, butter, sugar, and salt to a boil in a large saucepan. Add the flour all at once and cook, stirring constantly, until the dough begins to stick to the sides of the pan and all of the starch taste is cooked out. Remove from the heat, place the dough in the bowl of a stand mixer, and mix at low speed until the steam dissipates.

Add the eggs one at a time, beating at medium speed and blending completely after each addition. Pipe 2 inches apart in the desired shape and size onto the baking sheet. Bake until golden brown, about 10 to 15 minutes. Reduce the oven temperature to 350°F and bake until fully set and crisp, about 10 minutes. Take the puffs out of the oven and let cool on the baking sheet.

For the filling, pick through the crabmeat and discard any shell fragments. In a mixing bowl, combine the crabmeat, cream cheese, hard-boiled eggs, mayonnaise, Dijon mustard, onion, celery, Hatch Peppers, cilantro, lime juice, pepper powder, salt, and pepper and mix gently but thoroughly.

To assemble, slit the puffs horizontally and spoon the crab filling carefully into the puffs. Serve immediately.

Devilish Deviled Eggs

makes 20 deviled eggs

10 eggs, at room temperature

½ cup mayonnaise

Juice of 1 Melissa's Meyer Lemon

1 teaspoon yellow mustard

1 tablespoon finely chopped sun-dried tomatoes

1 teaspoon Melissa's Hatch Pepper Powder, mild or hot

Kosher salt to taste

Bring a large pot of water to a boil. Using a spoon, gently lower the eggs into the boiling water. Return the water to a boil and cook for 12 minutes. Cover, remove from the heat, and set aside for 5 minutes. Run cold water over the eggs until cool. Peel the eggs and cut in half lengthwise. Remove the yolks and place them in a bowl. Using a fork, mash the yolks. Add the mayonnaise, lemon juice, mustard, sun-dried tomatoes, pepper powder, and salt to taste and stir gently until mixed. Fill the egg whites with the egg yolk mixture and serve or chill in the refrigerator for up to 6 hours.

Crab & Hatch Pepper Jalapeño Poppers

makes 16 poppers

Cooking spray or vegetable oil

8 ounces (1 cup) lump crabmeat

3 Melissa's Hatch Peppers, roasted, peeled, stemmed, seeded, and diced *(see Hatch Pepper Essentials, page 12)*

4 cups grated mozzarella cheese

16 large jalapeño peppers

Preheat the oven to 400°F or a grill to medium-high. If baking, lightly coat a baking sheet with cooking spray or oil.

Pick through the crabmeat and discard any shell fragments. In a bowl, combine the crabmeat, Hatch Peppers, and mozzarella and mix well. Make a lengthwise slit in each jalapeño and carefully remove the seeds and veins. Carefully fill each jalapeño with the crab mixture. Place the jalapeños on the baking sheet or on a piece of foil on the grill and cook until the jalapeños begin to get tender, about 7 to 10 minutes. Serve hot.

Steamed Hatch Pepper– Seasoned Artichokes

makes 2 servings

2 large artichokes

2 Melissa's Seedless Lemons

2 limes

3 cloves Melissa's Peeled Garlic, halved

1 teaspoon kosher salt

1 tablespoon Melissa's Hatch Pepper Seasoning

Remove the stems of the artichokes and cut off the top ⅓ of each artichoke. Pull off any loose leaves and discard.

Pour about 2 inches of water into a pot. Place a steamer basket in the bottom of the pot. Bring the water to a simmer and add the artichokes stem sides down. Cut the lemons and limes in half, squeeze the juices over the artichokes, and drop the fruit into the water. Add the garlic to the water and season the artichokes with the salt and pepper seasoning.

Cover the pot and steam the artichokes for about 35 to 40 minutes or until a knife can be inserted easily into the base of the artichokes.

Remove from the pot and serve with garlic butter, chipotle mayonnaise, or your favorite dipping sauce.

Spicy Stuffed Mushrooms

makes 4 to 6 servings

Canola or olive oil spray

12 large button mushrooms

2 tablespoons extra-virgin olive oil

1 cup minced Melissa's Perfect Sweet Onion (about 1 onion)

1 Melissa's Hatch Pepper, roasted, peeled, stemmed, seeded, and chopped (2 tablespoons)
(see Hatch Pepper Essentials, page 12)

⅓ cup minced celery

1 clove Melissa's Peeled Garlic, minced

½ cup shredded Parmesan cheese

4 tablespoons (½ stick) unsalted butter, melted

¼ cup panko breadcrumbs

Kosher salt and freshly ground pepper to taste

Preheat the oven to 350°F. Spray a baking sheet with canola oil.

Remove the stems from the mushrooms and reserve the stems and caps. Place the mushroom caps open sides up on a baking sheet, spray with canola oil, and bake until the mushrooms are cooked through and tender, about 10 minutes. Remove from the oven and set aside.

Mince the reserved mushroom stems. In a sauté pan, heat the olive oil over medium heat. Sauté the onion until caramelized. Add the mushroom stems, Hatch Pepper, celery, and garlic and sauté for 3 minutes. Remove from the heat. Add the Parmesan, butter, breadcrumbs, and salt and pepper to taste and mix well. Let cool.

Stuff the mushroom caps with the filling and bake until heated through, about 7 to 8 minutes.

Sloppy Soyrizo Sliders

makes 10 to 12 sliders

2 tablespoons extra-virgin olive oil

2 tablespoons unsalted butter

½ Melissa's Perfect Sweet Onion, diced (about ½ cup)

Kosher salt and freshly ground pepper to taste

1 (12-ounce) package Melissa's Soyrizo

1 (14-ounce) can diced tomatoes

2 Melissa's Hatch Peppers, roasted, peeled, stemmed, seeded, and chopped *(see Hatch Pepper Essentials, page 12)*

¼ cup hickory-smoked barbecue sauce

10 to 12 Hawaiian sweet dinner rolls

Sliced cheese *(optional)*

In a sauté pan, heat the olive oil and melt the butter. Add the onion and salt and pepper to taste and sauté until the onion is caramelized. Add the Soyrizo and cook, stirring often, for 5 minutes. Mix in the tomatoes, Hatch Peppers, and barbecue sauce and bring to a simmer. Cook until completely heated through and the mixture thickens a bit. It should be a little saucy.

Cut the dinner rolls in half horizontally. Place equal amounts of the filling on the bottom halves of the rolls, add cheese if desired, and top with the remaining halves of the dinner rolls. Serve and enjoy.

Almost Meaty 7-Layer Dip

makes 8 to 10 servings

GUACAMOLE

6 avocados

2 Roma tomatoes, diced

½ Melissa's Perfect Sweet Onion, diced (about ½ cup)

1 serrano pepper, minced

2 cloves Melissa's Peeled Garlic, minced

⅛ teaspoon kosher salt

1 lime

DIP

2 (12-ounce) packages Melissa's Soy Taco

2 (8.8-ounce) packages Melissa's Steamed Six Bean Medley

2 cups sour cream

6 Roma tomatoes, diced

1 (12-ounce) jar Melissa's Hatch Salsa

2 cups shredded sharp cheddar cheese

1 (6½-ounce) can sliced black olives

3 scallions, ends trimmed and white and pale green parts sliced

Chips or crudités, for serving

For the guacamole, cut the avocados in half, remove the seeds, and scoop the pulp into a mixing bowl. Add the tomatoes, onion, serrano pepper, garlic, and salt. Cut the lime in half and squeeze the juice into the bowl. Using a potato masher, crush and mix everything together.

For the dip, prepare the Soy Taco following the package instructions. In a bowl, mix the Soy Taco and beans and spread evenly over the bottom of a glass 9 by 13-inch dish. Layer evenly with the guacamole, sour cream, tomatoes, salsa, and cheddar. Mix the olives and scallions in a small bowl and sprinkle over the layers. Serve with chips or crudités.

Layered Hatch Pepper Hummus Dip *with* Toasted Pita Chips

makes 6 to 8 servings

PITA CHIPS

6 whole pita rounds

Olive oil for brushing

Kosher salt and freshly ground black pepper to taste

HUMMUS

2 (9-ounce) packages Melissa's Peeled & Steamed Chickpeas

⅔ cup tahini

Juice of 1 Melissa's Seedless Lemon

6 Melissa's Hatch Peppers, roasted, peeled, stemmed, and seeded *(see Hatch Pepper Essentials, page 12)*

2 cloves Melissa's Peeled Garlic

1 pinch kosher salt

1 (3-ounce) package Melissa's Pine Nuts

1 (7½-ounce) jar Melissa's Italian Style Basil Pesto

8 Melissa's Veggie Sweet Mini Peppers, sliced into rounds

4 Melissa's Mini Cucumbers, diced

1 cup Mini San Marzano Tomatoes

½ cup feta cheese, crumbled

¼ cup grated Parmesan cheese

¾ cup sliced black olives

Fresh chopped cilantro, for garnish

For the pita chips, preheat the oven to 350°F. Cut the pita into triangles. Brush with olive oil on each side and sprinkle with salt and pepper to season. Bake for 8 to 10 minutes or until toasted.

For the hummus, place the chickpeas, tahini, lemon juice, Hatch Peppers, garlic, and salt in a food processor and blend until smooth.

In a dry sauté pan, add the pine nuts and toast them until golden brown, about 3 minutes, watching and stirring so they don't burn.

Spread the hummus evenly over the bottom of a glass 9 by 13-inch dish. Layer evenly with the pine nuts, pesto, sweet peppers, cucumbers, tomatoes, feta, Parmesan, and black olives. Sprinkle with the cilantro and serve with the pita chips.

Hatch Pepper Hummus

makes about 1½ cups

1 (9-ounce) package Melissa's Peeled & Steamed Chickpeas

⅓ cup tahini

Juice of ½ Melissa's Seedless Lemon

3 Melissa's Hatch Peppers, roasted, peeled, stemmed, and seeded
(see Hatch Pepper Essentials, page 12)

1 clove Melissa's Peeled Garlic

1 pinch kosher salt

Olive oil, for garnish

Melissa's Hatch Pepper Powder, mild or hot, to taste, for garnish

Warm pita bread or crudités, for serving

Place the chickpeas, tahini, lemon juice, Hatch Peppers, garlic, and salt in a food processor and blend until smooth. Place the hummus in a serving bowl, drizzle with olive oil, and sprinkle with pepper powder. Serve with warm pita bread or crudités.

Sweet, Smoky, & Spicy Party Nuts

makes 6 to 8 servings

Cooking spray

2 egg whites

1 tablespoon granulated sugar

2½ teaspoons Melissa's Hatch Pepper Powder, mild or hot

1½ cups smoked almonds

1½ cups butter toffee peanuts

1½ cups shelled pistachios

1½ cups cashew halves

1 tablespoon canola oil

Preheat the oven to 275°F. Lightly spray a baking sheet with cooking spray.

In a large bowl, whisk together the egg whites, sugar, and pepper powder. Add the almonds, peanuts, pistachios, and cashews and mix well to coat. Stir in the canola oil. Place the nuts in a single layer on the baking sheet. Bake, stirring every 10 minutes, until the nuts are lightly toasted, about 30 minutes. Remove the baking sheet from the oven and place on a wire rack. Stir the nuts, spread in a single layer, and cool on the baking sheet.

HATCH PEPPER

SALADS

Spring Mix & Berry Salad

Spring Mix & Berry Salad

makes about 6 servings

VINAIGRETTE

¼ cup red wine vinegar

1 tablespoon Dijon mustard

1 teaspoon honey

8 leaves fresh basil, cut into ribbons

2 tablespoons canola oil

⅛ teaspoon kosher salt

⅛ teaspoon freshly ground pepper

SALAD

10 cups (about 10 ounces) spring mix

1 cup strawberries, sliced

1 cup blueberries

1 cup raspberries

½ red onion, thinly sliced (about ½ cup)

½ (17.63-ounce) package Melissa's Cooked Quinoa, crumbled

½ cup goat cheese, crumbled

1 cup Melissa's Red Hatch Pepper Pecans

For the vinaigrette, whisk all of the vinaigrette ingredients in a bowl and set aside.

For the salad, combine the spring mix, strawberries, blueberries, raspberries, onion, and quinoa in a large bowl and toss to mix. Add the vinaigrette, toss to mix, and sprinkle with the goat cheese and pecans.

Hatch Caesar Salad *with* Hatch Pepper Polenta Croutons

makes 4 to 6 servings

DRESSING

1 pasteurized egg

½ cup Melissa's Hatch Salsa

½ cup extra-virgin olive oil

½ cup grated Parmesan cheese

2 cloves Melissa's Peeled Garlic

1 anchovy fillet in olive oil

Juice of 1 Melissa's Meyer Lemon

3 tablespoons red wine vinegar

1 tablespoon Dijon mustard

2 teaspoons Worcestershire sauce

⅛ teaspoon kosher salt

⅛ teaspoon freshly ground pepper

CROUTONS

1 tablespoon extra-virgin olive oil

1 tablespoon unsalted butter

1 (16-ounce) package Melissa's Hatch Pepper Polenta, cut into ¾-inch cubes

SALAD

1 head romaine, rinsed and cut into bite-size pieces

1 (10-ounce) package Melissa's Baby Heirloom Tomatoes, halved

½ cup shaved Parmesan cheese

For the dressing, bring 3 cups water to a boil in a saucepan, place the entire egg in the boiling water, and boil for 1 minute. Remove the egg from the water and let cool.

Crack the cooled egg into a blender, add the salsa, olive oil, Parmesan, garlic, anchovy, lemon juice, vinegar, mustard, Worcestershire sauce, salt, and pepper, and blend until smooth. Chill until ready to serve the salad.

For the croutons, heat the olive oil and melt the butter in a sauté pan, add the polenta, and sear on two sides until crisp, turning only once when they begin to brown. Remove to paper towels to drain and let cool.

For the salad, toss all of the salad ingredients in a large bowl and serve on 4 to 6 salad plates. Sprinkle with the croutons and top with the dressing.

Tropical Spinach Salad *with* Strawberry Balsamic Vinaigrette

makes 4 to 6 servings

VINAIGRETTE

1 cup fresh strawberries, hulled

1 tablespoon balsamic vinegar

1 tablespoon Melissa's Hatch Pepper Powder, mild or hot

1½ teaspoons brown sugar

Kosher salt and freshly ground pepper to taste

SALAD

8 cups (about 10 ounces) fresh baby spinach, washed and patted dry

1 cup fresh blueberries

1 cup fresh strawberries, hulled and quartered

1 cup walnuts, lightly toasted

½ cup crumbled blue cheese

For the vinaigrette, combine the strawberries, vinegar, pepper powder, and brown sugar in a blender. Season with salt and pepper to taste, process until smooth, and set aside.

For the salad, toss all of the salad ingredients in a large bowl, add the desired amount of the vinaigrette, and toss gently to mix. Adjust seasonings and serve.

Grilled Salsa Salad

makes 8 to 10 servings

1 (14-ounce) mango

6 Roma tomatoes (about
1½ pounds), halved

1 Melissa's Perfect Sweet Onion,
sliced (about 1 cup)

3 cloves Melissa's Peeled
Garlic

3 limes, halved

1 avocado, halved and pitted

Extra-virgin olive oil

1 tablespoon chopped
fresh cilantro

1 tablespoon Melissa's Hatch
Pepper Powder, mild or hot

1 pinch kosher salt

1 head butter lettuce, leaves
separated

Preheat a grill to medium-high.

Cut the cheeks off the mango by standing the mango on the stem end on a cutting board and cutting on each side about ¼ inch from the center. Discard the center section.

Brush the mango, tomatoes, onion, garlic, limes, and avocado lightly with olive oil, place them cut sides down on the grill, and grill until grill marks are formed. Set the limes aside, peel the avocado, and peel the mango if desired. Chop the grilled fruit and vegetables, place in a bowl, and toss gently to mix. Squeeze the limes over the salsa, add the cilantro, pepper powder, and salt, and toss gently to mix. Serve in the lettuce leaves.

Stone Fruit & Spring Mix Salad

makes 6 to 8 servings

8 cups (about 8 ounces) spring mix

2 nectarines, sliced

2 plums, sliced

3 Melissa's Mini Cucumbers, diced

1 large yellow bell pepper, stemmed, seeded, and sliced

1 large red bell pepper, stemmed, seeded, and sliced

½ cup seasoned rice vinegar

½ cup extra-virgin olive oil

1 tablespoon Melissa's Hatch Pepper Powder, mild or hot

1 teaspoon freshly ground black pepper

Kosher salt to taste

In a large bowl, combine the spring mix, nectarines, plums, cucumbers, yellow bell pepper, and red bell pepper and toss to mix.

In a small bowl, whisk together the vinegar, olive oil, pepper powder, black pepper, and salt to taste. Pour over the salad, toss to mix, and serve.

Hatch Pepper Shrimp & Orzo Salad

makes 4 to 6 servings

1 pound raw shrimp, peeled and deveined

2 tablespoons Melissa's Hatch Pepper Seasoning

1 lime, halved

8 ounces orzo

Olive oil, for the orzo

1½ cups seedless grapes, halved (about 12 ounces)

½ cup crumbled blue cheese

½ teaspoon ground Melissa's My Grinder® Organic Rainbow Peppercorns

Preheat a grill to medium.

In a bowl, season the shrimp with the pepper seasoning, squeeze the lime juice over them, and stir. Let the shrimp marinate for 5 minutes.

Grill the shrimp, turning once, until opaque, about 5 to 7 minutes. Cool completely.

Meanwhile, cook the orzo until al dente according to the package instructions and drain well. Place the orzo in a bowl, toss with a small amount of olive oil, and cool completely.

Add the shrimp, grapes, and blue cheese to the orzo and season with the ground pepper.

Mixed Grains Salad

makes 8 to 10 servings

SALAD

1 (10-ounce) package Mini San Marzano Tomatoes, sliced

6 scallions, trimmed and thinly sliced

2 bunches Italian parsley, finely chopped

½ cup finely chopped fresh mint

1 (6-ounce) package Melissa's Organic Farro, cooked and cooled

1 (8-ounce) package Melissa's Quinoa, cooked, cooled, and seasoning packet discarded

1 (6-ounce) package Melissa's Organic Red Quinoa, cooked and cooled

1 (10-ounce) package Melissa's Organic Shelled Edamame

DRESSING

1 Melissa's Hatch Pepper, roasted, peeled, stemmed, and seeded *(see Hatch Pepper Essentials, page 12)*

1 clove Melissa's Peeled Garlic

½ cup extra-virgin olive oil

¼ cup apple cider vinegar

Kosher salt and freshly ground pepper to taste

For the salad, layer the tomatoes, scallions, parsley, and mint in a large bowl and toss to mix. Add the farro, quinoa, red quinoa, and edamame and mix well.

For the dressing, combine the Hatch Pepper, garlic, olive oil, and vinegar in a blender. Add salt and ground pepper to taste and process until emulsified.

To assemble, add the dressing to the salad and toss to mix well.

Caprese & Hatch Pepper Salad

makes 4 to 6 servings

6 tablespoons balsamic vinegar

6 tablespoons packed brown sugar

2 pounds (about 2) heirloom tomatoes, sliced

1 pound fresh buffalo mozzarella cheese, sliced

¼ cup packed whole fresh basil leaves, rinsed and dried

1 teaspoon Melissa's Hatch Pepper Powder, mild or hot

Kosher salt and finely ground pepper to taste

In a small heavy saucepan, heat the vinegar and brown sugar over medium heat, stirring constantly, until the brown sugar is dissolved. Simmer for 1 minute and set the balsamic reduction aside to cool.

On a platter, layer 1 tomato slice, 1 mozzarella slice, and 1 basil leaf, slightly overlapping the layers. Sprinkle with pepper powder and season with salt and pepper to taste. Repeat the layers until all of the ingredients are used, starting a new row as needed. Drizzle with the cooled balsamic reduction and serve.

Grilled Veggie & Hatch Pepper Macaroni Salad

makes 6 to 8 servings

1 Melissa's Perfect Sweet Onion, sliced (about 1 cup)

2 large carrots, trimmed and halved lengthwise

2 tablespoons extra-virgin olive oil

Melissa's Hatch Pepper Seasoning to taste

Freshly ground pepper to taste

1 pound small elbow macaroni, cooked, drained, and rinsed with cold water

2 Melissa's Hatch Peppers, roasted peeled, stemmed, seeded, and chopped *(see Hatch Pepper Essentials, page 12)*

1 pint cherry or pear tomatoes, halved

3 Melissa's Mini Cucumbers, trimmed, quartered lengthwise, and chopped

2 (6½-ounce) jars marinated artichoke hearts, drained

1 small can black olives, drained

2 (3-ounce) packages Melissa's Pine Nuts, toasted

½ cup raisins

Juice of ½ Melissa's Seedless Lemon

1 tablespoon smoked paprika

½ cup crumbled feta cheese

1¼ cups Italian dressing

Preheat a grill to medium-high. Brush the onion and carrots with the olive oil and sprinkle with pepper seasoning and ground pepper to taste. Grill just until grill marks form; the carrots should still be crisp. Cool completely and chop the vegetables.

In a large bowl, combine the macaroni, Hatch Peppers, tomatoes, cucumbers, artichokes, olives, pine nuts, raisins, lemon juice, and paprika and mix well. Stir in the onion and carrots. Add the feta and dressing, toss to mix, and adjust the seasonings. Serve or refrigerate for up to 5 days.

Kickin' Organic Farro-Stuffed Avocado Bowls

makes 10 to 12 servings

1 (6-ounce) package Melissa's Organic Farro

2 cups chicken or vegetable broth

1 organic red bell pepper, finely diced

1 organic carrot, finely diced

1 organic jalapeño pepper, stemmed, seeded, deveined, and minced

½ cup Melissa's Hatch Salsa

6 organic avocados

2 organic limes

Melissa's My Grinder® Organic Rainbow Peppercorns

½ cup Mexican crema

¼ cup chopped organic cilantro, for garnish (optional)

Prepare the farro according to the package instructions, substituting the broth for the water. Let cool to room temperature.

In a mixing bowl, combine the farro, bell pepper, carrot, jalapeño, and salsa.

Cut the avocados into halves and remove the pits. Cut the limes into halves and squeeze the juice over the avocados. Season the avocados with a few grindings of peppercorns and arrange on a platter. Spoon the farro mixture into the avocado halves, drizzle equal portions of the crema on top of each, and garnish with cilantro if desired.

Ambrosia Salad *with* Heat

makes about 6 servings

3 tangerines, peeled and sectioned

8 ounces (about 8) fresh strawberries, hulled and quartered

2 bananas, peeled and sliced

1 pineapple, peeled, cored, and cubed

1½ cups Melissa's Dried Tart Cherries

2 jalapeño peppers, stemmed, seeded, and minced, divided

3 cups heavy cream

2 teaspoons Melissa's Green Hatch Pepper Powder, mild or hot

½ cup granulated sugar

½ cup powdered sugar, sifted

1 teaspoon pure vanilla extract

2 vanilla beans

2 cups mini marshmallows

1½ cups Melissa's Dried Coconut Chips, lightly toasted

Place the bowl of a stand mixer in the freezer to chill.

In a large bowl, combine the tangerines, strawberries, bananas, pineapple, dried cherries, and half the jalapeños, mix gently, and set aside.

In the chilled mixing bowl, combine the cream, pepper powder, granulated sugar, powdered sugar, and vanilla extract. Split the vanilla beans in half lengthwise, scrape the tiny seeds into the mixing bowl, and discard the pods. Whip the mixture until stiff peaks form.

In a large parfait dish, layer a third or half each of the tangerine mixture, marshmallows, coconut chips, and whipped cream mixture and repeat the layers until all of the ingredients are used. Sprinkle with the remaining jalapeños and serve.

BREADS

Hatch Pepper & Cheddar Cornbread

Hatch Pepper & Cheddar Cornbread

makes 6 to 8 servings

Cooking spray

1½ cups yellow cornmeal

¼ cup all-purpose flour

2 tablespoons granulated sugar

1 teaspoon baking powder

½ teaspoon baking soda

¼ teaspoon Melissa's Hatch Pepper Seasoning

1 Melissa's Hatch Pepper, roasted peeled, stemmed, seeded, and diced *(see Hatch Pepper Essentials, page 12)*

1 cup whole milk

1 cup sour cream

2 tablespoons unsalted butter, melted

1 large egg

¾ cup shredded sharp cheddar cheese

Preheat the oven to 400°F. Spray the bottom and sides of a 9-inch baking dish or cast-iron skillet with cooking spray.

In a medium bowl, whisk together the cornmeal, flour, sugar, baking powder, baking soda, and pepper seasoning and set aside.

In a small bowl, whisk together the Hatch Pepper, milk, sour cream, butter, and egg. Add the mixture to the cornmeal mixture, whisk until mixed, and mix in the cheddar.

Pour the batter into the baking dish and bake until a wooden pick inserted near the center comes out clean, about 25 to 30 minutes. Loosen the edge of the bread by running a knife between the bread and dish. Cut into wedges or squares and serve warm or at room temperature.

Hatch Pepper Buttermilk Biscuits *with* Honey Butter

makes 12 biscuits

HONEY BUTTER

8 tablespoons (1 stick) unsalted butter, softened

¼ cup honey

1 Melissa's Hatch Pepper, roasted, peeled, stemmed, seeded, and diced *(see Hatch Pepper Essentials, page 12)*

BISCUITS

4 cups all-purpose flour

1 tablespoon baking powder

½ teaspoon baking soda

2 teaspoons salt

8 tablespoons (1 stick) ice-cold butter, cut into cubes

3 Melissa's Hatch Peppers, roasted, peeled, stemmed, seeded, and diced *(see Hatch Pepper Essentials, page 12)*

1¾ cups buttermilk

4 tablespoons (½ stick) butter, melted, for brushing

For the honey butter, combine all of the honey butter ingredients in a mixing bowl and whisk until well mixed. The honey butter may be refrigerated for up to 1 week but bring to room temperature before serving.

For the biscuits, preheat the oven to 400°F. Grease a baking sheet.

In a mixing bowl, whisk together the flour, baking powder, baking soda, and salt. Add the cold butter one cube at a time, using your hands to incorporate the butter into the flour mixture until it resembles coarse crumbs. Stir in the Hatch Peppers and slowly add the buttermilk, mixing just until fully incorporated.

On a floured surface, shape the dough into a ball. Roll out into a rectangle and fold the dough over. Roll out again, fold over, and roll out into a ½-inch-thick rectangle. Cut out biscuits using a 2- or 3-inch ring cutter, place the biscuits on the baking sheet about 1 inch apart, and brush the tops with the melted butter. Bake until golden brown, about 15 to 20 minutes. Serve with the honey butter.

Hatch Pepper &
Cheese–Stuffed Flatbread

makes 12 to 14 flatbreads

1 cup warm water

1 (¼-ounce) envelope
(2¼ teaspoons) active dry yeast

1 teaspoon granulated sugar

3 cups all-purpose flour

1 tablespoon kosher salt

4 tablespoons extra-virgin
olive oil, divided

1 egg

1 tablespoon water

3 Melissa's Hatch Peppers, roasted
peeled, stemmed, seeded, and
diced *(see Hatch Pepper Essentials,
page 12)*

½ cup shredded sharp cheddar
cheese

⅓ cup shredded Parmesan cheese

In a small bowl, combine the warm water, yeast, and sugar and stir gently to dissolve the yeast. Let stand in a warm place until it starts to foam, about 5 to 10 minutes.

In the bowl of a stand mixer fitted with a dough hook, combine the flour and salt. Pour the yeast mixture into the bowl and mix at low speed until the flour is fully incorporated and the dough starts to come together. Mix at medium speed until the dough gathers into a ball. Add 2 tablespoons of the olive oil and pulse a few times to incorporate the oil. Turn the dough out onto a lightly floured surface and knead it until smooth and elastic. Shape the dough into a ball, put it in a bowl oiled with the remaining 2 tablespoons olive oil, and turn the dough to coat completely with oil. Cover the bowl with plastic wrap or a damp towel and let rise in a warm place until doubled in size, about 1 hour.

Preheat the oven to 350°F. Grease a large baking sheet or line with parchment paper.

Divide the dough into 24, 26, or 28 portions and roll out each portion to make a 4-inch circle, about ⅛ inch thick. In a bowl, whisk together the egg and 1 tablespoon water and brush over the edges of the circles. Divide the Hatch Peppers and cheddar evenly among half of the circles, top with the remaining circles, and crimp the edges with a fork to seal. Place the flatbreads on the baking sheet, brush the tops with the egg mixture, and sprinkle with the Parmesan. Bake until completely cooked through, about 30 minutes.

Hatch Pepper Pecan & Tart Cherry Challah Bread

makes 12 to 14 servings

2 (¼-ounce) envelopes (4½ teaspoons) active dry yeast

6½ ounces warm water (¾ cup plus 1 tablespoon)

1¼ ounces granulated sugar (about 2¾ tablespoons)

2 tablespoons canola oil

2 large eggs, divided

2 cups all-purpose flour

⅔ cup Melissa's Red Hatch Pepper Pecans, chopped

1 (3-ounce) package Melissa's Dried Tart Cherries

1 pinch kosher salt

Splash of water

In a large bowl, dissolve the yeast in the warm water. Stir in the sugar and mix in the canola oil and 1 of the eggs. Add the flour, pecans, dried cherries, and salt and knead for 8 to 10 minutes. Cover the dough with plastic wrap and let rise in a warm place for 20 minutes.

Preheat the oven to 350°F. Line a baking sheet with parchment paper.

Punch down the dough to release any air bubbles, divide the dough into three equal portions, and roll each portion into a long rope. Braid the ropes, place on the baking sheet, and set aside to proof for 15 minutes.

In a small bowl, whisk together the splash of water and remaining egg. Brush the mixture all over the dough and bake until golden brown, about 18 to 20 minutes.

Sweet Potato Bread
with Hatch Pepper
Compound Butter

makes 8 to 10 servings

BREAD

Butter and granulated sugar, for loaf pans

2 Melissa's Sweet Potatoes, peeled, boiled, and mashed

2 (3-ounce) packages Melissa's Dried Apricots, chopped

1¾ cups sifted all-purpose flour

1 cup granulated sugar

½ cup packed brown sugar

8 tablespoons (1 stick) unsalted butter, melted

⅓ cup whole milk

2 large eggs

1 teaspoon baking soda

½ teaspoon ground Melissa's Whole Nutmeg

½ teaspoon finely ground Melissa's Canela (about 1 cinnamon stick)

1 pinch kosher salt

COMPOUND BUTTER

1 pound (4 sticks) unsalted butter, softened

2 Melissa's Hatch Peppers, roasted, peeled, stemmed, seeded, and chopped
(see Hatch Pepper Essentials, page 12)

1 pinch kosher salt

For the bread, preheat the oven to 350°F. Grease the bottom and sides of two 5 by 9-inch loaf pans with butter and dust with sugar.

In the bowl of a stand mixer, combine the sweet potatoes, apricots, flour, granulated sugar, brown sugar, butter, milk, eggs, baking soda, nutmeg, canela, and salt. Beat until mixed, divide evenly between the two loaf pans, and bake until a wooden pick inserted near the center comes out clean, about 1 hour. Let stand to cool in the pans for 15 to 20 minutes and then invert onto a wire rack to cool.

For the compound butter, combine all of the compound butter ingredients in a bowl and mix well. Can be stored in the refrigerator for up to 2 weeks.

To serve, slice the bread, spread with some of the butter, and enjoy.

Hatch Pizza Dough

makes 4 to 6 servings

2 to 2½ cups bread flour

1 (¼-ounce) envelope
(2¼ teaspoons) active dry yeast

1½ teaspoons granulated sugar

3 cloves Melissa's Peeled Garlic,
minced

1 teaspoon dried oregano

2 tablespoons extra-virgin olive oil

1 teaspoon Melissa's Red Hatch
Pepper Powder, mild or hot

1 teaspoon Melissa's Green Hatch
Pepper Powder, mild or hot

¾ cup warm water

1 teaspoon kosher salt

In the bowl of a stand mixer fitted with a dough hook, combine 1 cup of
the flour, yeast, sugar, garlic, oregano, olive oil, red pepper powder, green
pepper powder, and water and mix at low speed until well mixed. Continue
mixing and add the salt and enough additional flour until the dough is
only slightly sticky.

Preheat a grill to 500°F using the indirect heat method or preheat the oven
to the highest temperature. While preheating the grill or oven, place a pizza
stone on the grill away from the flame or in the oven.

On a lightly floured surface, roll out the dough to the desired shape and
thickness. Spread your desired sauce over the dough and add your favorite
toppings. Place the pizza on the pizza stone and grill or bake until the pizza
is heated through and crispy on the bottom and the cheese is melted, about
8 to 10 minutes. Cut into wedges and serve.

HATCH PEPPER

SIDES

Lobster Mac & Cheese with Hatch Peppers

Lobster Mac & Cheese
with Hatch Peppers

makes about 4 servings

2 tablespoons unsalted butter

2 tablespoons all-purpose flour

1¼ cups whole milk

1 tablespoon dry mustard

2 teaspoons smoked paprika

1 large egg

1 tablespoon Worcestershire sauce

1½ cups shredded cheddar-Jack cheese

1½ cups shredded Gouda cheese

2 Melissa's Hatch Peppers, roasted, peeled, stemmed, seeded, and chopped
(see Hatch Pepper Essentials, page 12)

8 ounces cooked lobster meat

8 ounces elbow macaroni, cooked and drained

Kosher salt and freshly ground pepper to taste

In a large saucepan, melt the butter, add the flour all at once, and cook over medium-high heat, stirring constantly, for 2 minutes. Whisk in the milk, dry mustard, and paprika and cook, stirring frequently, until thickened, about 5 minutes.

Beat the egg in a medium bowl. Stir in about ½ cup of the milk mixture and pour the egg mixture into the saucepan. Stir in the Worcestershire sauce, add the cheddar-Jack and Gouda, and whisk until the cheese is melted. Stir in the Hatch Peppers and lobster.

Combine the macaroni and sauce in a bowl, season with salt and pepper to taste, and mix gently.

Roasted Hatch Pepper Navy Beans

makes 8 to 10 servings

3 tablespoons extra-virgin olive oil

1 unsmoked ham hock, scored

1 large Melissa's Perfect Sweet Onion, diced (about 1 cup)

4 ribs celery, trimmed and diced

2 cups diced Roma tomatoes

1 cup diced red bell pepper

4 cloves Melissa's Peeled Garlic, minced

½ teaspoon Mexican oregano

Freshly ground pepper to taste

2 smoked ham hocks, scored

12 Melissa's Hatch Peppers, roasted, peeled, stemmed, seeded, and diced *(see Hatch Pepper Essentials, page 12)*

1 pound navy beans, sorted and rinsed

16 cups chicken broth

In a large stockpot, heat the olive oil over medium-high heat, add the unsmoked ham hock, and brown it on both sides. Add the onion, celery, tomatoes, bell pepper, garlic, oregano, and ground pepper to taste. Add the smoked ham hocks and cook, stirring constantly, for 3 minutes. Add the Hatch Peppers, beans, and broth, bring to a boil, and then reduce the heat. Cover and simmer until the beans are tender, about 2 hours. Remove 2 cups of the bean mixture, purée in a blender, and stir back into the beans. Adjust the seasonings and serve.

Shredded Brussels Sprouts Slaw

makes 6 to 8 servings

2 pounds (about 28) fresh Brussels sprouts, shredded

2 carrots, shredded

1 leek stalk, trimmed and thinly sliced

4 Melissa's Hatch Peppers, roasted, peeled, stemmed, seeded, and finely diced *(see Hatch Pepper Essentials, page 12)*

2 cloves Melissa's Peeled Garlic, minced

¾ cup Greek yogurt

¼ cup milk

Juice of 1 Melissa's Seedless Lemon

⅓ cup granulated sugar

1½ tablespoons seasoned rice vinegar

1 tablespoon white wine vinegar

½ teaspoon kosher salt

⅛ teaspoon freshly ground pepper

In a large bowl, combine the Brussels sprouts, carrots, leek, Hatch Peppers, and garlic and toss to mix.

In a medium bowl, combine the Greek yogurt, milk, lemon juice, sugar, rice vinegar, wine vinegar, salt, and pepper and mix well. Pour over the salad, toss to mix, and cover. Chill for 1 to 2 hours to allow the flavors to marry.

Hatch Pepper Esquites

makes 3 to 4 servings

HATCH PEPPER BUTTER

1 pound (4 sticks) unsalted butter, softened

3 Melissa's Hatch Peppers, roasted, peeled, stemmed, seeded, and finely diced
(see Hatch Pepper Essentials, page 12)

CORN

4 ears corn with husks

2 tablespoons vegetable oil

Kosher salt and freshly ground pepper to taste

½ cup queso ranchero

¼ cup mayonnaise

Juice of ½ lime

½ tablespoon Melissa's Hatch Pepper Powder, mild or hot

¼ cup Mexican crema

Cilantro for garnish, chopped

For the butter, blend the ingredients in a bowl until well mixed, shape into a log on a piece of plastic wrap, and refrigerate until ready to use.

For the corn, preheat a grill to medium or the oven to 350°F. Place the corn with husks on a baking sheet and bake until the corn is tender, about 40 minutes. Let cool, then remove the husks from the corn.

Combine the vegetable oil and salt and pepper to taste in a large bowl and coat each ear of corn with the oil mixture. Grill the corn on the grill or bake on a baking sheet in the oven until slightly charred, about 5 minutes. Using a sharp knife, cut the corn off the cobs into a large bowl, toss with a mixture of 2 ounces of the Hatch Pepper Butter, queso, mayonnaise, lime juice, and pepper powder, and adjust the seasonings. Top each serving with Mexican crema and garnish with cilantro.

Roasted Mexican Street Corn

makes 4 to 6 servings

6 ears corn with husks

4 tablespoons (½ stick) unsalted butter

4 Melissa's Hatch Peppers, roasted, peeled, stemmed, seeded, and finely diced
(see Hatch Pepper Essentials, page 12)

6 tablespoons mayonnaise

2 tablespoons all-purpose flour

½ cup milk

¼ cup heavy cream

1½ cups shredded Monterey Jack cheese

½ teaspoon Melissa's Red Hatch Pepper Powder, mild or hot

½ teaspoon Melissa's Green Hatch Pepper Powder, mild or hot

½ cup crumbled Cotija cheese

½ cup chopped fresh cilantro

2 limes, cut into wedges, for serving

Preheat the oven to 350°F.

Place the corn in the husks on a baking sheet and bake until the corn is tender, about 25 minutes. Turn on the broiler and place the cobs about 6 inches from the heat. Broil just until slightly charred.

In a saucepan, melt the butter, add the corn and Hatch Peppers, and stir in the mayonnaise, flour, milk, and cream. Simmer, stirring constantly, until heated through, about 2 minutes. Stir in the Monterey Jack, simmer until the cheese is melted, about 3 to 4 minutes, and stir in the red and green pepper powders.

Brush the charred cobbs with the cream sauce. Sprinkle with the Cotija and cilantro, and serve with the lime wedges.

Baked Jicama Fries

makes 2 to 4 servings

1 Melissa's Jicama, peeled and cut into sticks

2 teaspoons extra-virgin olive oil

½ teaspoon garlic salt

½ teaspoon garlic powder

½ teaspoon Melissa's Green Hatch Pepper Powder, mild or hot

½ teaspoon onion powder

½ teaspoon smoked paprika

Preheat the oven to 425°F.

In a bowl, toss all of the ingredients until the jicama is well coated. Arrange in a single layer on a baking sheet and bake until crispy, about 30 to 35 minutes. Serve with your favorite dipping sauce.

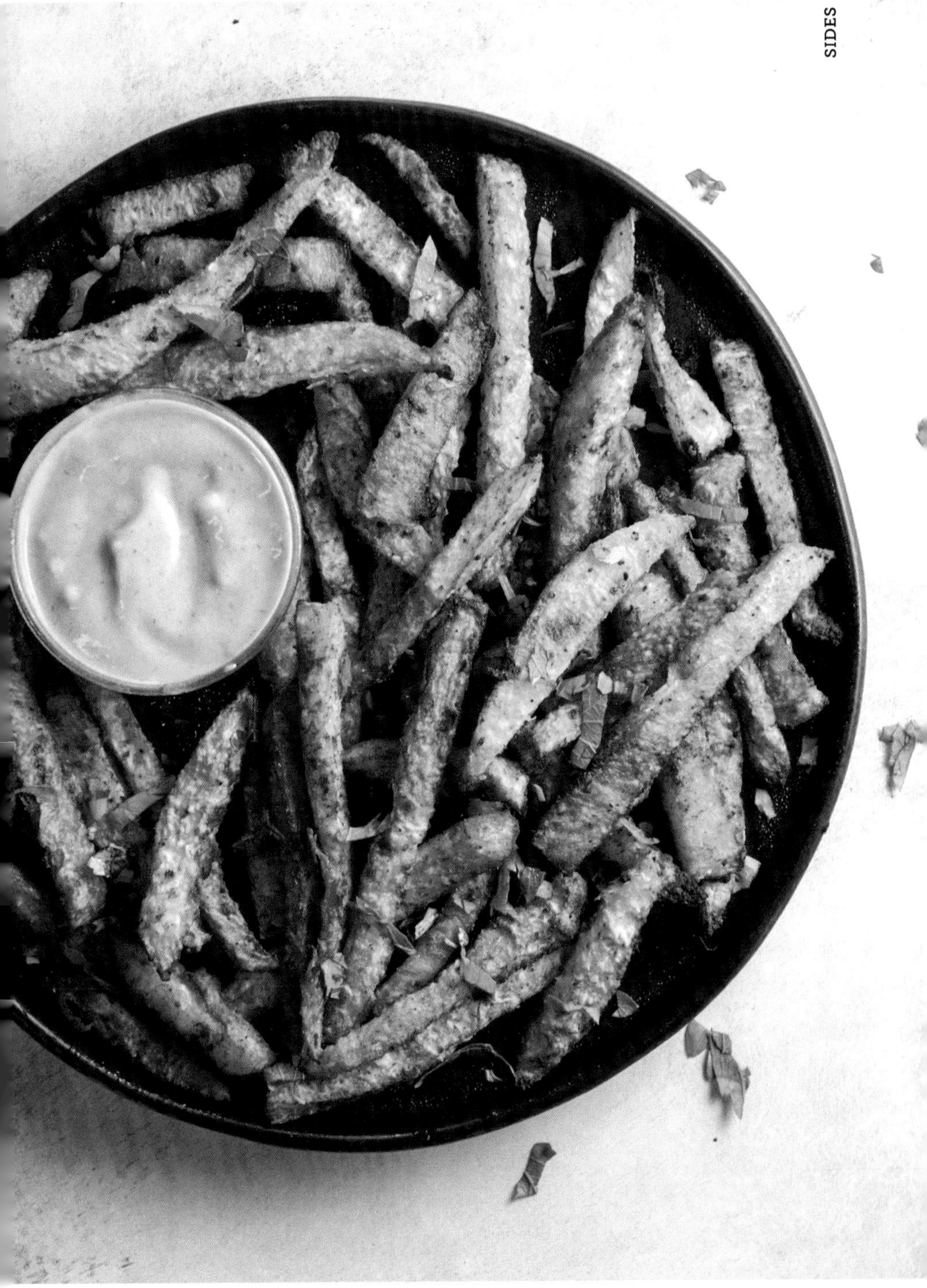

Roasted Kale Sprouts & Cauliflower *with* Hatch Pepper and Fresh Turmeric

makes 6 to 8 servings

6 tablespoons extra-virgin olive oil

Juice of 1 lime

1 Melissa's Hatch Pepper, peeled, stemmed, seeded, and diced *(see Hatch Pepper Essentials, page 12)*

1 tablespoon fresh turmeric, peeled and minced

1 teaspoon turmeric powder

1 head white cauliflower, cut into florets

2 (5-ounce) packages Melissa's Kale Sprouts, cut into halves

Kosher salt and freshly ground pepper to taste

Preheat the oven to 425°F.

In a mixing bowl, whisk together the olive oil, lime juice, Hatch Pepper, fresh turmeric, and turmeric powder. Add the cauliflower, kale sprouts, and salt and pepper to taste and toss to coat the vegetables well. Arrange in a single layer on a baking sheet, and roast until the vegetables are tender, about 15 to 20 minutes. Serve hot.

Boiler Onion Skewers

makes 3 to 4 skewers

1 pound Melissa's Boiler Onions

3 or 4 bamboo skewers, soaked in water

1 lime

Melissa's Green Hatch Pepper Powder, mild or hot, to taste

Garlic salt

Trim the stem ends from the onions, place the onions in a microwave-safe bowl, and cover them with water. Cover the bowl with plastic wrap, microwave on high for 2 minutes, and uncover.

Using a paring knife, cut most of the way through the root end of 1 onion and peel toward the stem end. Peel the rest of the onion using your hands. Repeat the procedure with the remaining onions.

Preheat a grill to medium-high.

Thread the onions onto the skewers. Cut the lime into halves and squeeze the juice over the onions. Season the onions with pepper powder to taste and garlic salt to taste, arrange the skewers on the grill, and grill, turning frequently, until the onions are tender, about 10 to 15 minutes.

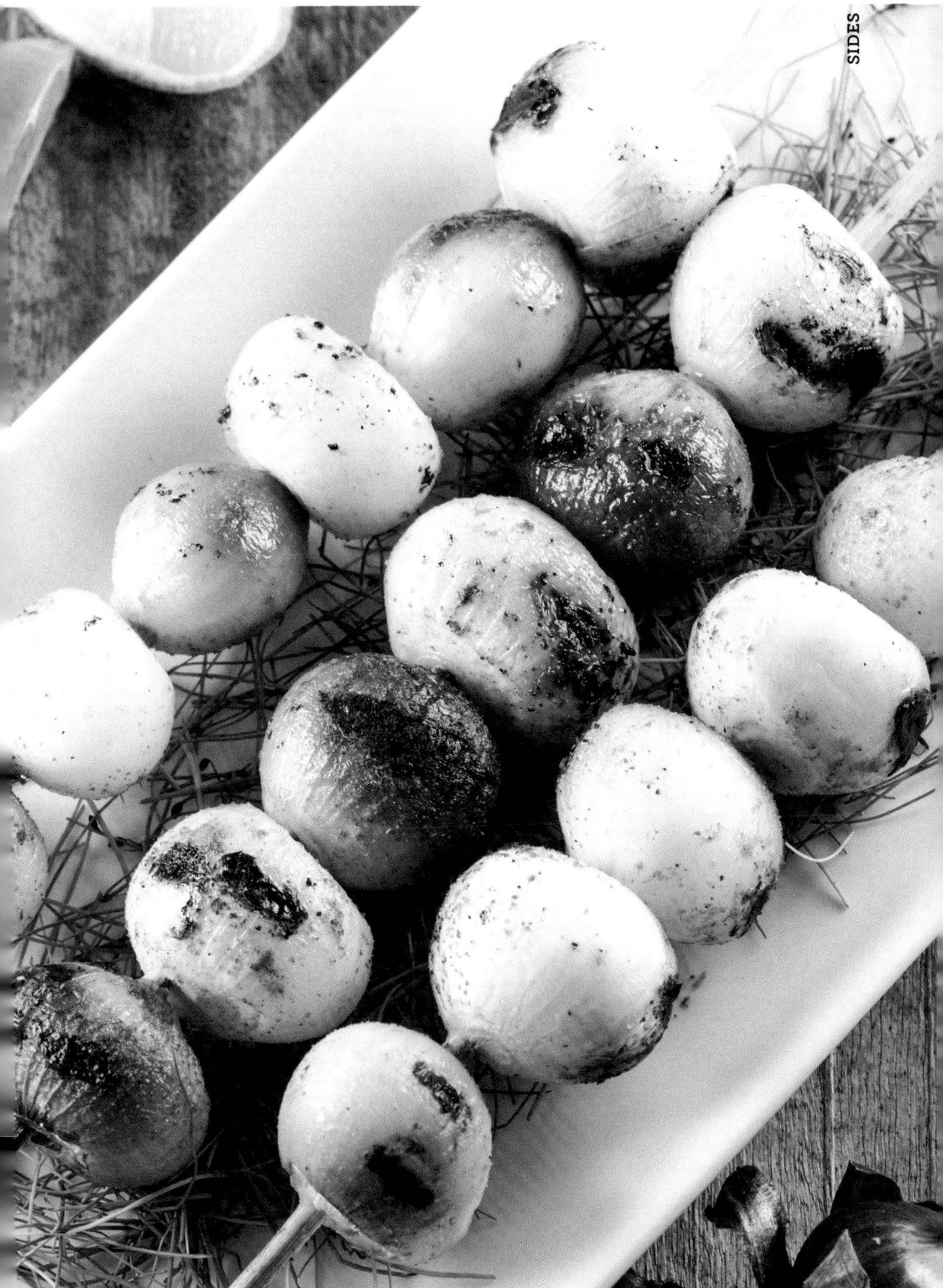

Potato & Cauliflower Bake *with* Hatch Pepper Sauce

makes 6 to 8 servings

1½ pounds (about 16) Melissa's Baby Dutch Yellow® Potatoes (DYPs®), halved

Kosher salt to taste

1 small head cauliflower, cut into florets

2 tablespoons extra-virgin olive oil

Freshly ground pepper to taste

2 tablespoons unsalted butter, for baking dish

⅓ cup heavy cream

3 cups shredded sharp cheddar cheese

3 Melissa's Dried Hatch Pepper Pods, stemmed and seeded

4 cloves Melissa's Peeled Garlic

Preheat the oven to 425°F.

In a large pot, combine the potatoes and enough water to cover, bring to a boil, and season generously with salt. Reduce the heat, simmer just until the potatoes are tender, about 10 minutes, and drain.

Meanwhile, combine the cauliflower, olive oil, and salt and pepper to taste in a bowl, arrange in a single layer on a baking sheet, and roast just until the cauliflower is tender, about 10 to 15 minutes.

Butter the bottom and sides of a 9 by 13-inch baking dish.

In a large bowl, combine the potatoes, cauliflower, and salt and pepper to taste and mix well. Spoon into the baking dish, pour the cream over the mixture, and sprinkle with the cheddar. Bake until heated through and the cheese is melted, about 10 to 15 minutes.

Combine the dried Hatch Pepper pods and enough water to cover in a saucepan, bring to a boil, and then simmer for 5 minutes. Remove from the heat, and drain the Hatch Peppers. Place them with the garlic in a blender, and season with salt to taste. Blend the mixture and add enough water to make the sauce smooth and at your desired consistency.

Serve the vegetables topped with the sauce.

Fried Smashed Malt Vinegar Potatoes

makes 4 to 6 servings

1 pound (about 12) Melissa's Baby Dutch Yellow® Potatoes (DYPs®)

1 pound (about 12) Crimson & Gold Potatoes

Kosher salt to taste

Canola oil, for frying

¾ cup malt vinegar

1 tablespoon granulated garlic

3 teaspoons Melissa's Hatch Pepper Powder, mild or hot

Freshly ground pepper to taste

In a large saucepan, combine the potatoes and enough cold water to cover, bring to a boil, and season generously with salt. Cook until the potatoes are tender, about 20 to 25 minutes, and drain. Pat the potatoes dry and smash them to ¼- to ½-inch thickness.

In a high-sided sauté pan, pour enough canola oil to reach 1 inch up the side and heat the oil to 365°F. Carefully add a batch of the potatoes without overcrowding the pan, and fry until crisp and golden brown, about 5 minutes. Drain the potatoes on paper towels. Drizzle each batch with an equal amount of the malt vinegar, sprinkle with equal portions of the granulated garlic and pepper powder, and season with ground pepper to taste. Repeat the procedure with the remaining potatoes.

Hatch Pepper Green Rice

makes 6 to 8 servings

2 tablespoons olive oil

½ cup diced onion (about ½ onion)

2 cups long grain white rice

1 Melissa's Hatch Pepper,
peeled, stemmed, and seeded
(see Hatch Pepper Essentials, page 12)

1 bunch cilantro

1 quart chicken broth

In a saucepan, heat the olive oil and sauté the onion until translucent, about 3 minutes. Add the rice and sauté, stirring constantly, until lightly browned, about 5 minutes.

In a blender, combine the Hatch Pepper, cilantro, and broth and process until blended. Add to the rice mixture, bring to a boil, and then reduce the heat to low. Cover and steam until the rice is tender, about 20 minutes.

Deconstructed DYPs® & Mini San Marzano Tomato Hash *with* Hatch Pepper

makes 4 to 6 servings

2 tablespoons unsalted butter

4 tablespoons extra-virgin olive oil, divided

1 Melissa's Perfect Sweet Onion, very thinly sliced (about 1 cup)

Kosher salt and freshly ground pepper to taste

1½ pounds Melissa's Pee Wee Dutch Yellow® Potatoes (DYPs®)

1 (10-ounce) package Mini San Marzano Tomatoes

Canola oil, for frying

1 Melissa's Green Hatch Pepper, roasted, peeled, stemmed, seeded, and diced *(see Hatch Pepper Essentials, page 12)*

1 Melissa's Red Hatch Pepper or red bell pepper, roasted, peeled, stemmed, seeded, and diced *(see Hatch Pepper Essentials, page 12)*

½ bunch fresh cilantro, chopped

Preheat the oven to 425°F.

In a saucepan, melt the butter and heat 2 tablespoons of the olive oil over medium heat. Add the onion, season with salt and pepper to taste, and sauté the onion, stirring occasionally, until caramelized, about 8 to 10 minutes.

Place the potatoes in a bowl, add the remaining 2 tablespoons olive oil and salt and pepper to taste, and mix well. Arrange the potatoes in a single layer on a baking sheet, reserving the olive oil in the bowl, and roast the potatoes until golden brown, about 15 minutes.

Add the tomatoes to the reserved oil and carefully coat them with the oil. Arrange the tomatoes on a baking sheet and roast until lightly charred, about 8 to 10 minutes.

When the potatoes are slightly cooled, flatten them with the back of a spatula. Coat the bottom of a frying pan with canola oil, heat over medium heat, and carefully add the potatoes in a single layer. Fry the potatoes until crisp, about 7 minutes, and drain on paper towels.

Place a ring mold in the center of a salad plate. Layer equal portions of the potatoes, tomatoes, and green and red Hatch Peppers in the mold and press gently. Carefully remove the mold and repeat the procedure until all of the potatoes, tomatoes, and Hatch Peppers are used. Top each serving with caramelized onion and sprinkle each with a small amount of cilantro.

HATCH PEPPER
ENTRÉES

Grilled Bone-In Rib-Eye Steaks with Grilled Fruit Salsa Topper

Grilled Bone-In Rib-Eye Steaks *with* Grilled Fruit Salsa Topper

makes 2 servings

SALSA

1 Melissa's White Peach, halved and pitted

1 Melissa's Pluot, halved and pitted

1 slice Melissa's Yellow Watermelon

1 green apple, halved and cored

1 mango, halved and pitted

Cooking spray

1 Melissa's Hatch Pepper, roasted, peeled, stemmed, seeded, and diced *(see Hatch Pepper Essentials, page 12)*

8 Melissa's Red Muscato™ Grapes, halved

8 Melissa's Green Muscato™ Grapes, halved

¼ cup finely diced Melissa's Perfect Sweet Onion (about ¼ onion)

3 Melissa's Basil Leaves, cut into ribbons

⅛ teaspoon kosher salt

⅛ teaspoon freshly ground pepper

Juice of 1 lime

STEAKS

2 bone-in rib-eye steaks

2 tablespoons Melissa's Hatch Pepper Seasoning

1 avocado, sliced

For the salsa, preheat a grill to medium-high.

Spray the peach, pluot, watermelon, apple, and mango with cooking spray and grill until grill marks form, about 3 minutes. Turn the fruit over, grill until grill marks form, about 3 minutes, and cool completely.

Dice the peach, pluot, and apple. Peel the watermelon and mango and dice.

In a bowl, combine the diced fruit, Hatch Pepper, red and green grapes, onion, basil, salt, and ground pepper, add the lime juice, and toss gently.

For the steaks, rub the steaks with the pepper seasoning, grill until the desired doneness is reached, and let rest for 5 minutes.

To serve, plate a steak, top with half the avocado slices, and finish with the salsa.

Grilled Surf & Turf
with Kale Sprout Slaw

makes 4 servings

SLAW

12 ounces Melissa's Kale Sprouts, stemmed

3 tablespoons extra-virgin olive oil, divided

¼ teaspoon kosher salt

¼ teaspoon freshly ground pepper

¾ cup Melissa's Pepitas

⅛ teaspoon Melissa's Hatch Pepper Seasoning

½ head napa cabbage, shredded

3 Melissa's Mini Cucumbers, trimmed, halved lengthwise, and thinly sliced

1½ cups Melissa's Dried Cranberries

Store-bought coleslaw dressing to taste

STEAK AND LOBSTER

4 bone-in rib-eye steaks

2 tablespoons Melissa's Hatch Pepper Seasoning

2 tablespoons granulated garlic

4 teaspoons freshly ground pepper

4 lobster tails

Olive oil to taste, for drizzling

4 tablespoons (½ stick) butter, melted

2 tablespoons thinly sliced fresh basil

For the slaw, preheat the oven to 425°F.

In a bowl, combine the kale sprouts, 2 tablespoons of the olive oil, salt, and ground pepper and toss to coat the sprouts with the oil. Spread the sprouts on a baking sheet and roast until lightly charred, about 10 minutes. Cool completely, chop, and set aside.

In a sauté pan over medium heat, combine the pepitas, pepper seasoning, and remaining 1 tablespoon olive oil. Sauté, stirring frequently, until the pepitas are toasted, about 3 to 5 minutes.

In a large bowl, combine the cabbage, cucumbers, and dried cranberries. Stir in the kale sprouts, pepitas, and coleslaw dressing to taste and set aside.

For the steak and lobster, preheat a grill to medium-high.

Rub the steaks all over with the pepper seasoning, garlic, and ground pepper. Grill until medium-rare, about 4 minutes per side. Remove from the grill and set aside to rest.

Using kitchen shears, split the tops of the lobster shells and cut lengthwise about halfway through the meat. Drizzle with olive oil to taste and place cut side down on the hot grill. Grill until lightly charred, about 5 minutes. Turn over the lobster tails, brush with the butter, and sprinkle with the basil. Grill until the lobster is opaque, about 5 minutes.

To serve, plate some of the slaw and add a lobster tail and steak.

Hatch Pepper–Braised Short Ribs

makes 5 to 6 servings

3 pounds Korean-style short ribs

Kosher salt and freshly ground pepper to taste

4 tablespoons olive oil, divided

1 pound (about 8) Melissa's Fresh Tomatillos, husked and quartered

1 green bell pepper, chopped

½ cup diced onion (about ½ onion)

2 cloves Melissa's Peeled Garlic, chopped

6 Melissa's Hatch Peppers, roasted, peeled, and stemmed
(see Hatch Pepper Essentials, page 12)

½ bunch cilantro

1 quart chicken broth

Preheat the oven to 350°F.

Season the ribs with salt and ground pepper to taste. Let rest for about 30 minutes.

In a sauté pan over medium-high heat, heat 2 tablespoons of the olive oil, sear the ribs in the oil on all sides until browned, and remove from the pan. This step may be done on the grill, using less oil.

In a saucepan, heat the remaining 2 tablespoons olive oil and sauté the tomatillos, bell pepper, onion, garlic, Hatch Peppers, and cilantro in the oil until tender. Add the chicken broth.

With an immersion blender, blend the mixture until smooth.

In a baking dish, place the ribs, pour the tomatillo mixture evenly over the top, and cover tightly with plastic wrap and foil. Bake for 30 minutes and adjust seasonings if needed.

Big Game Chili

makes 6 to 8 servings

2 tablespoons extra-virgin olive oil

1 Melissa's Perfect Sweet Onion, diced (about 1 cup)

1 green bell pepper, chopped

1 red bell pepper, chopped

1 rib celery, chopped

1 clove Melissa's Peeled Garlic, minced

1½ pounds beef, cut into cubes

1⅛ teaspoons kosher salt, divided

2 (14½-ounce) cans peeled whole tomatoes

1 (8-ounce) can tomato sauce

2 (9-ounce) packages Melissa's Steamed Red Kidney Beans

2 tablespoons Melissa's Green Hatch Pepper Powder, mild or hot

1½ teaspoons ground cumin

¼ teaspoon freshly ground pepper

⅛ teaspoon ground cayenne pepper

Shredded cheddar-Jack cheese, for serving

Sour cream, for serving *(optional)*

In a stockpot, heat the olive oil, add the onion, green and red bell peppers, celery, garlic, beef, and ⅛ teaspoon of the salt, and sauté until the meat is browned, about 5 minutes. Add the whole tomatoes with juice, crushing the tomatoes with your hands. Stir in the tomato sauce, beans, pepper powder, cumin, ground pepper, cayenne pepper, and remaining 1 teaspoon salt. Bring to a boil, reduce the heat, and simmer gently, stirring frequently, until the beef is tender, about 45 minutes.

Serve the chili with cheddar-Jack cheese and sour cream if desired.

Hatch "Macadillo"

makes 6 to 8 servings

PICADILLO

2 tablespoons extra-virgin olive oil

1 pound ground beef

½ onion, diced (about ½ onion)

1 green bell pepper, diced

1 red bell pepper, diced

1 Melissa's Hot Hatch Pepper, roasted, peeled, stemmed, seeded, and chopped *(see Hatch Pepper Essentials, page 12)*

2 cloves Melissa's Peeled Garlic, chopped

2 tomatoes, diced

½ bunch cilantro, chopped

½ cup chicken broth

¼ cup tomato purée

1 bay leaf

1 teaspoon ground cumin

1 tablespoon Hatch Pepper Seasoning

Kosher salt and freshly ground pepper to taste

MAC AND CHEESE

1 tablespoon butter

½ onion, diced (about ½ onion)

2 cloves Melissa's Peeled Garlic, chopped

2 cups heavy cream

1 cup chicken broth

2 cups shredded cheddar cheese, divided

2 cups shredded Jack cheese, divided

1 pound elbow macaroni, cooked and drained

2 Melissa's Hatch Peppers, roasted, peeled, stemmed, seeded, and chopped *(see Hatch Pepper Essentials, page 12)*

Kosher salt and freshly ground pepper to taste

For the picadillo, heat the olive oil in a sauté pan over medium-high heat, add the ground beef, and cook, stirring to crumble, until browned; drain.

Add the onion, green and red bell peppers, Hatch Pepper, garlic, tomatoes, and cilantro and cook until the vegetables are tender, about 5 minutes. Stir in the broth, tomato purée, bay leaf, and cumin. Simmer for 20 minutes. Stir in the pepper seasoning, and season with salt and pepper to taste. Remove the bay leaf.

Preheat the oven to 350°F.

For the mac and cheese, melt the butter in a saucepan over medium-high heat, add the onion and garlic, and cook until translucent. Add the cream and broth, bring up to a simmer, and cook until slightly thickened, about 5 minutes.

Add 1½ cups each of the cheddar and Jack cheeses a handful at a time, whisking constantly and allowing the cheese to melt after each addition. Stir in the macaroni and Hatch Peppers, and season with salt and pepper to taste.

To assemble, combine the mac and cheese and picadillo in a large bowl and mix well. Spoon into a 9 by 13-inch baking dish, top with the remaining cheddar and Jack cheese, and bake until heated through and the cheese is melted, about 10 minutes.

Hatch Pepper Sloppy José Sliders

makes 6 to 8 servings

1 tablespoon extra-virgin olive oil

2 pounds ground beef

½ cup diced onion (about ½ onion)

2 cloves Melissa's Peeled Garlic, chopped

4 Melissa's Hatch Peppers, roasted, peeled, stemmed, seeded, and diced *(see Hatch Pepper Essentials, page 12)*

½ cup chopped cilantro

1 cup tomato purée

¾ cup tomato sauce

1 tablespoon brown sugar

Kosher salt and freshly ground pepper to taste

12 dinner rolls

In a sauté pan, heat the olive oil over medium-high heat, add the ground beef, onion, and garlic, and cook until the ground beef is browned, stirring to crumble; drain.

Add the Hatch Peppers, cilantro, tomato purée, tomato sauce, and brown sugar, reduce the heat, and simmer until the flavors marry, about 20 minutes. Season with salt and pepper to taste and serve over open-faced dinner rolls.

Hatch Pozole Verde

makes 4 to 6 servings

6 cups chicken broth

1 pound boneless, skinless chicken breasts

2 tablespoons extra-virgin olive oil

8 ounces (about 4) Melissa's Fresh Tomatillos, husked and quartered

1 green bell pepper, diced

¼ cup diced onion (about ¼ onion)

½ bunch cilantro

4 cloves Melissa's Peeled Garlic, chopped

3 Melissa's Hot Hatch Peppers, roasted, peeled, stemmed, seeded, and diced *(see Hatch Pepper Essentials, page 12)*

1 cup diced potatoes

1 cup chopped spinach

1 cup hominy

Kosher salt and freshly ground pepper to taste

Shredded cabbage, for garnish

Diced radishes, for garnish

In a large saucepan, bring the broth to a boil, add the chicken, and cook until cooked through, about 30 minutes. Remove the chicken from the broth and shred the chicken. Strain and reserve the broth.

In a saucepan, heat the olive oil and sauté the tomatillos, bell pepper, onion, cilantro, and garlic until tender.

In a blender, combine the reserved broth, Hatch Peppers, and tomatillo mixture and process until smooth. Return the mixture to the saucepan. Add the potatoes and simmer until the potatoes are tender. Add the shredded chicken, spinach, and hominy and bring to a boil. Season with salt and pepper to taste and serve garnished with cabbage and radishes.

Hatch Meat Loaf Adobada

makes 6 to 8 servings

GLAZE

1 tablespoon vegetable oil

¼ cup diced onion (about ¼ onion)

1 Melissa's Hot Hatch Pepper, roasted, peeled, stemmed, seeded, and chopped *(see Hatch Pepper Essentials, page 12)*

1 clove Melissa's Peeled Garlic, chopped

1 cup pineapple juice

1 cup tomato paste

¼ cup packed brown sugar

2 teaspoons kosher salt

1 teaspoon freshly ground pepper

2 tablespoons cold water

1 tablespoon cornstarch

MEAT LOAF

¼ pound bacon, chopped

1 tablespoon vegetable oil

¼ cup diced onion (about ¼ onion)

¼ cup diced green bell pepper

¼ cup diced red bell pepper

4 cloves Melissa's Peeled Garlic, chopped

2 Melissa's Hot Hatch Peppers, roasted, peeled, stemmed, seeded, and chopped *(see Hatch Pepper Essentials, page 12)*

¼ cup pineapple juice

2 tablespoons Worcestershire sauce

1 tablespoon achiote paste

1 tablespoon tomato paste

2 tablespoons Melissa's Hatch Pepper Powder, mild or hot

2 teaspoons kosher salt

1 teaspoon freshly ground pepper

1½ pounds ground beef

1 pound ground pork

2 eggs, beaten

1 cup breadcrumbs

For the glaze, heat the vegetable oil in a saucepan over medium-high heat and sauté the onion, Hatch Pepper, and garlic until tender, about 5 minutes. Add the pineapple juice, tomato paste, and brown sugar. Season with salt and pepper and mix well. Bring to a boil, reduce the heat to medium-low, and simmer for 5 minutes.

In a small bowl, mix the water and cornstarch to make a slurry and drizzle into the sauce, whisking constantly. Bring to a boil and set aside.

For the meat loaf, preheat the oven to 350°F.

Heat a sauté pan over medium-high heat, add the bacon, and sauté until crisp, about 5 minutes. Remove the bacon, reserving the drippings in the pan, and set the bacon aside. Add the vegetable oil to the drippings and then

add the onion, green and red bell peppers, and garlic. Cook until tender, about 5 minutes. Remove from the heat and stir in the bacon, Hatch Peppers, pineapple juice, Worcestershire sauce, achiote paste, tomato paste, pepper powder, salt, and pepper.

In a mixing bowl, combine the ground beef, ground pork, and sautéed vegetable mixture, add the eggs and breadcrumbs, and mix thoroughly.

Shape the mixture into a loaf on a baking sheet. Bake until a meat thermometer inserted near the center reads 165°F, about 1 hour. Brush with the glaze and serve.

Grape and Hatch Pepper–Stuffed Pork Chops

makes 2 servings

3 ½ cups Melissa's Red, Green, and Black Muscato™ Grapes, rinsed

1 Melissa's Hatch Pepper, roasted, peeled, stemmed, seeded, and chopped *(see Hatch Pepper Essentials, page 12)*

1 tablespoon granulated sugar

Juice of 2 Melissa's Seedless Lemons

Juice of 1 lime

½ cup red wine

1 tablespoon ground ginger

Kosher salt and freshly ground pepper to taste

2 bone-in pork chops

Preheat the oven to 350°F.

In a saucepan over medium-high heat, combine the grapes, Hatch Pepper, sugar, lemon juice, lime juice, wine, ginger, and salt and pepper to taste and bring to a boil. Reduce the heat and simmer, stirring frequently and smashing the grapes, for 20 minutes. Remove from the heat and cool slightly.

Using a sharp knife, cut a pocket in the side of each pork chop. Using a spoon, stuff the pork chops with some of the grape mixture.

Place the pork chops in a baking dish, top with the remaining grape mixture, and bake until a meat thermometer inserted near the center reads 150°F, about 20 minutes. Let rest for 5 minutes before serving.

Hatch Barbecue Pulled Pork

makes 8 to 10 servings

PORK

2 tablespoons paprika

2 tablespoons Melissa's Hatch Pepper Powder, mild or hot

1 teaspoon garlic powder

1 teaspoon onion powder

1 teaspoon dried oregano

2 tablespoons kosher salt

1 teaspoon freshly ground pepper

6 tablespoons packed brown sugar, divided

5 pounds pork butt

3 cups blended watermelon

5 cups chicken stock

3 Melissa's Mild Hatch Peppers, roasted, peeled, stemmed, seeded, and chopped *(see Hatch Pepper Essentials, page 12)*

1 onion, chopped (about 1 cup)

2 ribs celery, chopped

2 carrots, chopped

SAUCE

3 cups blended watermelon

3 Melissa's Hot Hatch Peppers, roasted, peeled, stemmed, seeded, and chopped *(see Hatch Pepper Essentials, page 12)*

2 tablespoons olive oil

½ medium onion, diced (about ½ cup)

2 cloves Melissa's Peeled Garlic, chopped

2 cups tomato purée

4 tablespoons Dijon mustard

½ cup packed brown sugar

1½ cups cider vinegar

2 cups reserved braising liquid, strained

8 to 10 dinner rolls, for serving

Coleslaw, for topping *(optional)*

For the pork, preheat the oven to 350°F.

Combine the paprika, pepper powder, garlic powder, onion powder, oregano, salt, pepper, and 2 tablespoons of the brown sugar in a bowl and mix well. Rub all over the pork and refrigerate in a covered bowl for 2 to 12 hours.

In a deep ovenproof pan, combine the watermelon, chicken stock, Hatch Peppers, onion, celery, carrots, and remaining 4 tablespoons brown sugar. Mix well. Add the pork and cover tightly. Bake until the pork is fork tender, about 2 to 3 hours. Shred the pork and reserve the braising liquid for the sauce.

For the sauce, purée the watermelon and Hatch Peppers in a blender until liquefied. In a saucepan over medium-high heat, heat the olive oil, add the onion and garlic, and sauté until tender, about 5 minutes. Add the watermelon mixture, tomato purée, mustard, brown sugar, vinegar, and reserved braising liquid, mix well, and simmer for 20 minutes.

To assemble, add the shredded pork to the sauce and cook until heated through, about 5 minutes. Slice each dinner roll and fill with the pork. Top with coleslaw if desired.

Octoberfest with a Twist

makes 2 servings

1 cup sauerkraut

½ (8-ounce) package Melissa's Steamed Baby Red Beets, finely diced

1 green apple, cored and finely diced

½ cup Dijon mustard

2 tablespoons honey

Melissa's Hatch Pepper Powder, mild or hot, to taste

2 beer 'n bratwurst "brats"

2 hot dog buns or rolls

Extra-virgin olive oil, for the buns

Preheat a grill to medium-high.

In a bowl, combine the sauerkraut, beets, and apple, mix well, and set aside.

In a small bowl, mix the mustard, honey, and pepper powder to taste and set aside.

Grill the brats, turning occasionally, until cooked through and lightly charred, about 20 minutes, and set aside.

Brush the insides of the buns with a small amount of olive oil, place on the grill oiled sides down, and grill until golden brown, about 45 seconds.

To assemble, place a bun on each of 2 plates, place the brats in the buns, and top each with equal amounts of the sauerkraut mixture. Drizzle with the mustard mixture and serve.

Sausage, Mushroom, & Hatch Pepper Kolaches

makes 16 kolaches

1 (¼-ounce) envelope (2 ¼ teaspoons) active dry yeast

½ cup warm water

2 cups whole milk

8 tablespoons (1 stick) unsalted butter, melted

4 eggs, divided

1 ¼ cups granulated sugar

2 teaspoons kosher salt

8 ½ cups all-purpose flour

Vegetable oil, for bowl

1 pound bulk sausage, crumbled and cooked

1 Melissa's Perfect Sweet Onion, sliced (about 1 cup), caramelized

6 ounces (about 18) button or cremini mushrooms, sliced and sautéed

2 Melissa's Hatch Peppers, roasted, peeled, stemmed, seeded, and diced *(see Hatch Pepper Essentials, page 12)*

1 thick slice cheddar cheese, cubed

1 thick slice mozzarella cheese, cubed

Melissa's Hatch Pepper Powder, mild or hot, to taste

In a small bowl, dissolve the yeast in the warm water and set aside.

In a saucepan over medium heat, bring the milk to a simmer. Remove from the heat.

In the bowl of a stand mixer fitted with a dough hook, combine the butter, 2 of the eggs, sugar, and salt and mix well. Add the dissolved yeast and milk and mix well. Add the flour gradually, mixing constantly. Continue mixing until well blended; the mixture will be sticky.

Place the dough in an oiled bowl, cover, and let the dough rise until doubled in size, about 1 hour. Punch down the dough, cover, and refrigerate for at least 4 hours.

Preheat the oven to 375°F. Spray a baking sheet with cooking spray.

Separate the dough into 16 balls, place the balls on the baking sheet, and press to flatten. Combine the sausage, onion, mushrooms, Hatch Peppers, cheddar, and mozzarella in a bowl and mix well. Place equal portions of the

mixture onto the center of each dough circle, pull up two sides, and pinch the edges to completely enclose the filling. Turn the kolaches seam sides down.

In a bowl, whisk together the remaining 2 eggs and pepper powder to taste. Brush the tops of the kolaches with the egg mixture and bake until golden brown, about 25 minutes.

Hatch Enchiladas Suizas

makes 1 quart salsa verde and 12 to 14 enchiladas

SALSA VERDE

2 tablespoons olive oil

8 Melissa's Fresh Tomatillos (about 1 pound), husked and quartered

½ yellow onion, diced (about ½ cup)

½ green bell pepper, diced

½ bunch cilantro, chopped

3 Melissa's Hot Hatch Peppers, roasted, peeled, stemmed, seeded, and diced *(see Hatch Pepper Essentials, page 12)*

1 clove Melissa's Peeled Garlic, chopped

2 cups chicken broth

½ cup heavy cream

½ cup sour cream

Kosher salt and freshly ground pepper to taste

ENCHILADAS

1 cup vegetable oil

12 corn tortillas

1½ pounds boneless, skinless chicken breasts, cooked and shredded

3 cups shredded Monterey Jack cheese, divided

Preheat the oven to 350°F.

For the salsa verde, heat the olive oil over medium heat in a saucepan and sauté the tomatillos, onion, bell pepper, cilantro, Hatch Peppers, and garlic until softened. Add the chicken broth and simmer until the vegetables are tender.

In a blender, process the vegetable mixture until smooth. Strain through a fine-mesh strainer. Return the sauce to the saucepan and bring to a simmer. Add the heavy cream and let reduce, stirring constantly, for 5 minutes. Stir in the sour cream and season with salt and pepper to taste. The sauce can be made ahead and refrigerated for up to 3 days before using if desired.

For the enchiladas, heat the vegetable oil in a sauté pan; it should be hot but not shimmering. Coat both sides of each tortilla in the oil to soften, remove to a plate, and blot gently with a paper towel.

In a mixing bowl, combine the shredded chicken and 1½ cups of the salsa verde; stir until all the chicken is coated.

Divide the chicken mixture among the 12 tortillas and sprinkle each with a small amount of Monterey Jack. Roll each tortilla to enclose the filling and place seam side down in a 9 by 13-inch baking dish.

Top the enchiladas with the remaining 2½ cups of salsa verde and remaining Monterey Jack. Bake until the sauce and cheese are bubbly, about 10 minutes. Serve immediately.

Hatch Shrimp & Andouille Sausage Gumbo

makes 10 to 12 servings

4 ounces vegetable oil (about ½ cup)

4 bone-in chicken thighs

3 ribs celery, diced

1 onion, diced (about 1 cup)

4 Melissa's Hatch Peppers, roasted, peeled, stemmed, seeded, and diced *(see Hatch Pepper Essentials, page 12)*

½ green bell pepper, diced

4 cloves Melissa's Peeled Garlic, minced

1 cup all-purpose flour

1½ quarts chicken broth

½ cup canned peeled whole tomatoes, blended

1 tablespoon kosher salt

1 teaspoon freshly ground black pepper

1 teaspoon dried oregano

2 bay leaves

1½ pounds andouille sausage, sliced diagonally

1½ pounds (16/20) shrimp, peeled and deveined

Hatch Pepper Green Rice *(page 85)*

In a saucepan over medium heat, heat the vegetable oil. Cook the chicken, turning once, until golden brown, about 10 minutes per side. Remove to a plate, reserving the pan drippings, and set the chicken aside.

Increase the heat to medium-high, add the celery, onion, Hatch Peppers, bell pepper, and garlic to the pan drippings, and sauté under tender, about 5 minutes. Add the flour and cook, stirring constantly, until light golden brown, about 5 minutes.

Add the broth, tomatoes, salt, pepper, oregano, and bay leaves and bring to a boil. Add the chicken, reduce the heat to medium, and cover. Cook until the chicken is cooked through, about 20 minutes. Add the sausage and shrimp, cover, and cook until the shrimp is opaque, about 15 minutes. Remove the bay leaves and serve over Hatch Pepper Green Rice.

Mexican-Style Shrimp Scampi *with* Green and Yellow Squash Noodles

makes 2 to 4 servings

2 green zucchini, trimmed

2 yellow zucchini, trimmed

2 tablespoons extra-virgin olive oil

2 tablespoons unsalted butter

3 cloves Melissa's Peeled Garlic, minced

1 Melissa's Hatch Pepper, roasted, peeled, stemmed, seeded, and diced *(see Hatch Pepper Essentials, page 12)*

1 pound raw shrimp, peeled and deveined

½ cup white wine

Melissa's Hatch Pepper Powder, mild or hot, to taste

2 tablespoons chopped fresh cilantro

1 lime, halved

Using the fine-blade spiralizer attachment of a stand mixer, cut the green and yellow zucchini according to the manufacturer's instructions for making noodles and set the noodles aside.

In a sauté pan, heat the olive oil and melt the butter, add the garlic and Hatch Pepper, and sauté until fragrant, about 30 seconds Add the shrimp in a single layer and add the wine. Bring just to a low boil and cook until opaque on one side, about 2 minutes. Turn over the shrimp and cook until the shrimp are opaque, about 1 to 2 minutes. Remove the shrimp to a plate, reserving the pan drippings, and sprinkle the shrimp with pepper powder to taste.

Stir the cilantro into the reserved drippings. Plate the zucchini noodles, add the shrimp, and pour the pan sauce over the shrimp and noodles. Squeeze the lime juice over the top.

Hatch Coctel de Camaron

makes about 4 servings

1 pound peeled and deveined shrimp, cooked

½ red onion, diced (about ½ cup)

½ bunch cilantro, chopped

1 tomato, diced

Juice of ½ lime

2 tablespoons ketchup

2 cups Clamato tomato cocktail

1 cucumber, seeded and diced

1 avocado, diced

1 Melissa's Hot Hatch Pepper, roasted, peeled, stemmed, seeded, and diced *(see Hatch Pepper Essentials, page 12)*

½ cup Melissa's Hatch Salsa

Kosher salt and freshly ground pepper to taste

Tortilla chips, for serving

In a large bowl, combine the shrimp, onion, cilantro, tomato, lime juice, ketchup, Clamato, cucumber, avocado, Hatch Pepper, and salsa and toss to mix. Season with salt and pepper to taste, chill for 1 hour, and serve with tortilla chips.

Creamy Hatch Polenta *with* Hatch Pepper Chili

makes 4 to 6 servings

POLENTA

2 tablespoons extra-virgin olive oil

½ Melissa's Perfect Sweet Onion, finely diced (about ½ cup)

1 (1-pound) package Melissa's Hatch Pepper Polenta, cubed

¾ cup chicken stock or broth

¼ cup heavy cream

CHILI

1 tablespoon extra-virgin olive oil

1 tablespoon unsalted butter

1 Melissa's Perfect Sweet Onion, finely diced (about 1 cup)

½ green bell pepper, finely diced

1 rib celery heart, finely diced

1 clove Melissa's Peeled Garlic, minced

½ teaspoon kosher salt

⅛ teaspoon freshly ground black pepper

1 Melissa's Hatch Pepper, roasted, peeled, stemmed, seeded, and diced *(see Hatch Pepper Essentials, page 12)*

1 (12-ounce) package Melissa's Soy Taco

1 (14½-ounce) can diced tomatoes

1 (9-ounce) package Melissa's Steamed Red Kidney Beans

4 ounces tomato sauce

1 tablespoon Melissa's Hatch Pepper Powder, mild or hot

1 teaspoon ground cumin

1 pinch ground cayenne pepper

For the polenta, heat the olive oil in a saucepan over medium-high heat and sauté the onion until translucent, about 5 minutes. Add the polenta and chicken stock. With a potato masher, mash the polenta to the consistency of mashed potatoes. Stir in the cream, remove from the heat, and set aside.

For the chili, heat the olive oil and melt the butter in a stockpot. Add the onion and cook, stirring frequently, for 2 minutes. Add the bell pepper, celery, and garlic, season with the salt and black pepper, and sauté until tender, about 5 minutes. Stir in the Hatch Pepper, Soy Taco, tomatoes, beans, tomato sauce, pepper powder, cumin, and cayenne pepper and bring to a boil. Reduce the heat to medium and simmer, stirring occasionally, until the flavors marry, about 30 minutes.

To serve, spoon equal portions of the polenta into each of 4 to 6 bowls, top with equal portions of the chili, and serve.

Peppers Tolucos

makes 6 servings

6 Melissa's Dried Hatch Pepper Pods

2 quarts water

½ cup cider vinegar

1 cup orange juice

1 pound Don Enrique® Piloncillo (3 cones), chopped

5 cloves Melissa's Peeled Garlic

1 teaspoon dried oregano

1 teaspoon dried thyme

4 ounces Melissa's Soyrizo

2 tablespoons canola oil

1 cup refried beans

Kosher salt to taste

12 ounces Manchego cheese, grated, divided

1 cup crema or sour cream

Preheat the oven to 350°F.

Slit each dried Hatch Pepper lengthwise and remove the seeds and veins without making additional cuts in the peppers. Bring the water to a boil in a stockpot over high heat, remove from the heat, and add the Hatch Peppers. Soak the peppers for 20 minutes or until softened.

In a saucepan over medium heat, combine the vinegar and orange juice and bring to a simmer. Add the piloncillo, garlic, oregano, and thyme and cook, stirring constantly, until the piloncillo is dissolved, about 5 to 7 minutes. Remove from the heat, add the softened Hatch Peppers, and soak until they feel fleshy, about 15 to 20 minutes.

While the peppers are soaking, sauté the Soyrizo in the canola oil in a skillet over medium heat until heated through. Stir in the beans, and season with salt to taste. Let the mixture cool.

Transfer the soaked peppers with a slotted spoon to a plate lined with paper towels to absorb any excess liquid, reserving the sauce in the pan. Strain the reserved sauce into a bowl and keep warm.

Stuff the peppers with equal portions of the Soyrizo mixture and 8 ounces of the Manchego, arrange seam sides down in a baking dish, and spoon crema over the top. Sprinkle with the remaining 4 ounces of Manchego and bake until the cheese is melted, about 15 minutes. Serve with the warm sauce.

Roasted Hatch Pepper & Onion Pasta

makes 4 to 6 servings

2 Melissa's Perfect Sweet Onions, sliced (about 2 cups)

2 tablespoons vegetable oil

2 cups roasted, peeled, stemmed, and seeded Melissa's Hatch Peppers *(see Hatch Pepper Essentials, page 12)*

3 cloves Melissa's Peeled Garlic, diced

1 (3-ounce) package sun-dried tomatoes, reconstituted in hot water for 15 minutes, drained

1 (14½-ounce) can crushed tomatoes

⅔ cup white wine

¼ cup extra-virgin olive oil

Sea salt and freshly ground black pepper

16 ounces penne pasta

⅓ cup Melissa's Pepitas, toasted

In a large sauté pan over medium-high heat, cook the onions in the vegetable oil until golden brown, about 7 minutes.

Cut the Hatch Peppers into strips about the size of the penne. Add the peppers and garlic to the onions and cook and stir for 1 minute. Stir in the sun-dried tomatoes. Add the crushed tomatoes, wine, and olive oil and bring to a boil. Reduce the heat to medium and simmer until the flavors marry, about 15 minutes. Season with salt and black pepper to taste.

Cook the penne according to the package instructions, drain, and add to the sauce. Add the pepitas and toss to mix.

Hatch Tacos de Papa

makes 8 to 10 tacos

2 pounds (about 20) Melissa's Baby Dutch Yellow® Potatoes (DYPs®)

1 tablespoon kosher salt, for the potatoes

1 cup chicken stock

8 tablespoons (1 stick) butter

2 Melissa's Mild Hatch Peppers, roasted, peeled, stemmed, seeded, and chopped *(see Hatch Pepper Essentials, page 12)*

2 Melissa's Hot Hatch Peppers, roasted, peeled, stemmed, seeded, and chopped *(see Hatch Pepper Essentials, page 12)*

Kosher salt and freshly ground pepper to taste

12 corn tortillas

Vegetable oil, for frying

2 cups shredded lettuce

1 tomato, diced

1 cup queso ranchero

In a large saucepan over medium-high heat, combine the potatoes and enough water to cover, add the salt, and bring to a boil. Reduce the heat to medium and simmer until the potatoes are tender, about 20 minutes. Drain the potatoes, return to the saucepan, and place the saucepan back on the warm burner.

In a separate saucepan over medium-high heat, heat the chicken stock and butter. Pour over the potatoes and mash to the desired consistency. Fold in the mild and hot Hatch Peppers and season with salt and pepper to taste.

Heat the tortillas for a few seconds each in a dry skillet or in the microwave and fill each with about 2 tablespoons of the potato mixture. Fold the tortillas and secure with a wooden pick.

Working in batches, fry the tacos in 1 inch of vegetable oil in a skillet over medium-high heat until golden brown, about 2 minutes per side, and drain on paper towels.

When the tacos have cool slightly, remove the wooden picks and fill the tacos with equal portions of the lettuce, tomato, and queso ranchero.

Hatch Pepper & Pepperoni Pizza

makes 4 to 6 servings

½ cup marinara sauce

1 store-bought pizza crust or 1 recipe Hatch Pizza Dough *(page 65)*

20 slices pepperoni

2 Melissa's Hatch Peppers, roasted, peeled, stemmed, seeded, and chopped *(see Hatch Pepper Essentials, page 12)*

¾ cup shredded sharp cheddar cheese

¾ cup shredded mozzarella cheese

½ teaspoon Melissa's Green Hatch Pepper Powder, mild or hot

½ teaspoon chopped fresh oregano

½ teaspoon chopped fresh basil

Preheat the oven to 500°F, placing a pizza stone in the oven while it preheats.

Spread the marinara sauce over the pizza crust and arrange the pepperoni on top of the sauce. Sprinkle with the Hatch Peppers, cheddar, mozzarella, pepper powder, oregano, and basil and bake, rotating every few minutes, until the pizza is lightly charred, about 10-12 minutes. Cut and serve.

HATCH PEPPER
SOUPS

Kickin' Crab & Grilled Corn Chowder

Kickin' Crab & Grilled Corn Chowder

makes 8 to 10 servings

8 tablespoons (1 stick) unsalted butter, divided

4 ears fresh corn, husks and silks removed

Kosher salt and freshly ground pepper to taste

8 ounces bacon, finely diced

1 Melissa's Perfect Sweet Onion, finely diced (about 1 cup)

8 cloves Melissa's Peeled Garlic, minced

4 shallots, minced

2 ribs celery, diced

1 teaspoon Melissa's Hatch Pepper Powder, mild or hot, or to taste

½ cup all-purpose flour

6 cups whole milk

2 cups heavy cream

2 bay leaves

2 large Yukon potatoes, peeled and diced

1 pound fresh crabmeat

Preheat a grill to medium-high.

Melt 4 tablespoons of the butter in a saucepan over medium heat and brush on the corn. Season the corn with salt and pepper to taste and grill until lightly charred on all sides. Remove from the grill and cool. Cut the corn from the cob into a bowl and set aside.

In a large stockpot over medium heat, sauté the bacon until crisp. Add the onion, garlic, shallots, celery, and pepper powder; cook, stirring frequently, for 5 minutes. Add the remaining 4 tablespoons butter and heat until melted. Stir in the flour and cook, stirring constantly, until smooth, about 3 minutes. Whisk in the milk and cream, add the bay leaves and potatoes, and bring to a boil. Reduce the heat to low, cover, and simmer until the potatoes are tender, about 15 minutes.

Remove the bay leaves from the chowder, stir in the crabmeat and corn, and adjust the seasonings. Serve hot.

Vegetarian Meatball Tortilla Soup

makes 8 to 10 servings

MEATBALLS

1 (12-ounce) package Melissa's Soyrizo

½ cup panko breadcrumbs

¼ cup grated Parmesan cheese

½ Melissa's Perfect Sweet Onion, minced (about ½ cup)

2 cloves Melissa's Peeled Garlic, minced

1 pinch kosher salt

1 pinch freshly ground pepper

2 tablespoons extra-virgin olive oil

SOUP

3 tablespoons extra-virgin olive oil

1 Melissa's Perfect Sweet Onion, finely diced (about 1 cup)

3 cloves Melissa's Peeled Garlic, minced

2 carrots, trimmed and chopped

2 ribs celery, trimmed and chopped

1 cup red enchilada sauce

1 (28-ounce) can stewed tomatoes

2 Melissa's Hatch Peppers, roasted, peeled, stemmed, seeded, and chopped *(see Hatch Pepper Essentials, page 12)*

1 green bell pepper, stemmed, seeded, and chopped

8 cups vegetable stock or broth

1 (3-ounce) package Melissa's Dry Roasted Sweet Corn

2 teaspoons dried Mexican oregano

2 teaspoons ground cumin

1 tablespoon Melissa's Hatch Pepper Powder, mild or hot

⅓ cup sherry

Juice of 1 lime, plus lime wedges, for garnish

Fresh fried tortilla strips, for garnish *(optional)*

Shredded cheddar cheese, for garnish *(optional)*

Avocado slices, for garnish

Cilantro, for garnish

For the meatballs, combine the Soyrizo, panko, Parmesan, onion, garlic, salt, and pepper in a bowl and mix well. Shape the mixture into about 14 balls. Heat the olive oil in a sauté pan, sear the meatballs on all sides, and set aside.

For the soup, heat the olive oil in a large saucepan over medium heat and

cook the onion, stirring constantly, until caramelized. Add the garlic, carrots, and celery and cook, stirring frequently, for 3 minutes. Add the meatballs and enchilada sauce and stir gently. Add the tomatoes, Hatch Peppers, bell pepper, vegetable stock, corn, oregano, cumin, pepper powder, and sherry and stir gently. Bring to a boil, simmer over medium-low heat for 30 minutes, and stir in the lime juice.

To serve, ladle the soup into soup bowls and, if desired, garnish with tortilla strips, cheddar, avocado, cilantro, and wedges of lime for spritzing.

Hatch Pepper Chicken Tortilla Soup

makes 8 to 10 servings

3 tablespoons extra-virgin olive oil

1 Melissa's Perfect Sweet Onion, finely diced (about 1 cup)

3 cloves Melissa's Peeled Garlic, minced

2 carrots, trimmed and chopped

2 ribs celery, trimmed and chopped

4 boneless, skinless chicken breasts, chopped

1 cup red enchilada sauce

1 (28-ounce) can stewed tomatoes

2 Melissa's Hatch Peppers, roasted, peeled, stemmed, seeded, and chopped *(see Hatch Pepper Essentials, page 12)*

1 green bell pepper, stemmed, seeded, and diced

8 cups chicken stock or broth

1 (3-ounce) package Melissa's Dry Roasted Sweet Corn

2 teaspoons dried Mexican oregano

2 teaspoons ground cumin

1 tablespoon Melissa's Hatch Pepper Powder, mild or hot

⅓ cup sherry

Juice of 1 lime, plus lime wedges, for garnish

Fresh fried tortilla strips, for garnish

Avocado slices, for garnish

Cilantro, for garnish

Shredded mozzarella cheese, for garnish *(optional)*

In a large saucepan, heat the olive oil over medium heat and cook the onion, stirring constantly, until caramelized. Add the garlic, carrots, and celery and cook, stirring frequently, for 3 minutes. Add the chicken, stir in the enchilada sauce, and add the tomatoes, Hatch Peppers, bell pepper, chicken stock, corn, oregano, cumin, pepper powder, and sherry and stir gently. Bring to a boil, simmer over medium-low heat for 30 minutes, and stir in the lime juice.

To serve, ladle the soup into soup bowls and garnish with tortilla strips, avocado, cilantro, and mozzarella if desired.

Hatch Clam Chowder

makes 12 servings

CLAMS

2 pounds fresh clams

8 cups cold water, divided

⅔ cup salt, divided

½ cup chicken broth

¼ cup water

6 cloves Melissa's Peeled Garlic, crushed

CHOWDER

8 tablespoons (1 stick) unsalted butter, divided

4 ears fresh corn, husks and silks removed

Freshly ground black pepper

8 ounces bacon, chopped

2 Melissa's Perfect Sweet Onions, diced (about 2 cups)

8 cloves Melissa's Peeled Garlic, minced

2 ribs celery, trimmed and finely chopped

2 Melissa's Hatch Peppers, roasted, peeled, stemmed, seeded, and chopped (*see Hatch Pepper Essentials, page 12*)

½ cup all-purpose flour

6 cups whole milk

2 cups heavy cream

2 bay leaves

2 Yukon gold potatoes, peeled and cut into ½-inch cubes

2 tablespoons Melissa's Red Hatch Pepper Powder, mild or hot

Freshly chopped cilantro, for garnish (*optional*)

Melissa's Hatch Salsa, for garnish (*optional*)

For the clams, inspect the clams to make sure they are tightly closed. Combine the clams, 4 cups of the cold water, and ⅓ cup of the salt in a large bowl and chill for 20 minutes. Discard any clams that float to the top. Using a slotted spoon or your hands, transfer the clams to a clean bowl, and repeat the soaking and discarding procedure. Brush the outsides of the clam shells with a vegetable brush to remove any remaining dirt.

Bring the broth, ¼ cup water, and garlic to a boil in a large skillet over medium-high heat. Add the clams and cover. Cook until all of the clams have opened, about 5 to 10 minutes, and immediately remove from the heat. Reserve some of the cooking liquid. Scoop the clam meat out of the shells and chop the meat if desired.

For the chowder, preheat a grill to medium-high. Melt 4 tablespoons of the butter in a saucepan over medium heat and brush on the corn. Season with pepper to taste and grill until lightly charred on all sides. Remove from the grill and let cool slightly. Cut the corn from the cob into a bowl and set aside.

In a large stockpot over medium heat, sauté the bacon until crisp. Add the onions, garlic, celery, and Hatch Peppers and cook, stirring frequently, until the onions are translucent, about 5 minutes. Add the remaining 4 tablespoons butter and heat until melted. Stir in the flour and cook, stirring constantly, until smooth, about 3 minutes. Whisk in the milk and cream. Add the bay leaves, potatoes, and pepper powder, and bring to a boil. Reduce the heat to low, cover, and simmer until the potatoes are tender, about 15 minutes.

Remove the bay leaves from the chowder, stir in the corn and clams, and simmer just until heated through. Adjust the seasonings and add some of the reserved cooking liquid for more clam flavor if desired. Garnish servings with cilantro and salsa if desired.

Lemon Drop Melon
Gazpacho *with* Grilled Shrimp

makes 6 to 8 servings

18 medium or large raw shrimp, peeled and deveined

Melissa's Green Hatch Pepper Powder, mild or hot, to taste

Sea salt to taste

Juice of 3 limes, divided

Cooking spray or olive oil, for the grill

½ Melissa's Lemon Drop Melon, peeled, seeded, and finely diced (about 2 cups)

6 Roma tomatoes, finely diced

2 Melissa's Enjoya Peppers or red bell peppers, stemmed, seeded, and finely diced

1 Melissa's Perfect Sweet Onion, finely diced (about 1 cup)

2 ribs celery, finely diced

4 Melissa's Mini Cucumbers, finely diced

2 serrano peppers, minced

6 cloves Melissa's Peeled Garlic, minced

½ teaspoon ground cumin

½ teaspoon dried oregano

3 cups tomato juice

½ cup balsamic vinegar

¼ cup extra-virgin olive oil

6 dashes Worcestershire sauce

Kosher salt and freshly ground pepper to taste

Preheat a grill to medium-high. Place the shrimp in a large bowl, season with pepper powder and sea salt to taste. Add a third of the lime juice and stir gently. Spray the grill with cooking spray or brush with olive oil. Grill the shrimp on both sides until grill marks are formed and the shrimp are opaque, about 2 minutes per side. Remove from the grill and set aside.

In a bowl, combine the melon, tomatoes, Enjoya Peppers, onion, celery, cucumbers, serrano peppers, garlic, cumin, oregano, tomato juice, vinegar, ¼ cup olive oil, and Worcestershire sauce. Season with kosher salt and ground pepper to taste. Add the remaining lime juice, mix well, and chill the gazpacho for at least 30 minutes.

To serve, ladle the gazpacho into soup bowls and hang 2 or 3 shrimp on the edge of each bowl.

Roasted Heirloom Tomato & Hatch Pepper Soup

makes 4 to 6 servings

3 pounds (about 3) fresh heirloom tomatoes

2 Melissas's Perfect Sweet Onions, peeled and quartered (about 2 cups)

6 cloves Melissa's Peeled Garlic

¼ cup extra-virgin olive oil

Kosher salt and freshly ground pepper to taste

6 Melissa's Hatch Peppers, roasted, peeled, stemmed, seeded, and chopped *(see Hatch Pepper Essentials, page 12)*

6 Don Enrique® Dried California Peppers (about 3 ounces), stemmed and seeded

4 cups chicken stock or broth

4 tablespoons (½ stick) unsalted butter

1 cup fresh basil leaves

Preheat the oven to 425°F.

Combine the tomatoes, onions, and garlic in a large bowl and toss with the olive oil and salt and pepper to taste. Arrange the vegetables in a single layer on a baking sheet and roast the vegetables until tender, about 30 minutes.

In a large stockpot, combine the roasted vegetables, Hatch Peppers, dried peppers, and chicken stock and bring to a boil. Simmer, stirring occasionally, until the peppers are reconstituted, about 20 minutes. Remove from the heat and add the butter and basil. Blend the soup using an immersion blender until smooth or carefully remove in batches to a blender and process until smooth. Serve hot.

Ramen Soup

makes 8 to 10 servings

2 tablespoons extra-virgin olive oil

1 Melissa's Perfect Sweet Onion, thinly sliced (about 1 cup)

3 carrots, julienned

2 ribs celery, thinly sliced

3 cloves Melissa's Peeled Garlic, minced

⅛ teaspoon kosher salt

⅛ teaspoon freshly ground pepper

6 Melissa's Baby Bok Choy, trimmed and chopped

3 stalks Melissa's Gai Lan, trimmed and chopped

1 cup button mushrooms, sliced

2 Melissa's Hatch Peppers, roasted, peeled, stemmed, seeded, and diced *(see Hatch Pepper Essentials, page 12)*

1 serrano pepper, sliced

5 cups chicken stock

¼ cup soy sauce

2 tablespoons sriracha

1 tablespoon seasoned rice vinegar

1 tablespoon fish sauce

1 package Melissa's Fresh Chinese Noodles, cooked

1 bunch fresh cilantro, chopped, for garnish

In a large stockpot, heat the olive oil and add the onion, carrots, celery, garlic, salt, and pepper. Cook for 5 minutes, stirring occasionally. Add the bok choy, gai lan, mushrooms, Hatch Peppers, and serrano pepper and stir to mix. Sauté for 3 minutes.

Add the chicken stock and bring to a boil. Simmer for 10 minutes, stirring occasionally. Add the soy sauce, sriracha, vinegar and fish sauce and stir. Simmer for 5 minutes, stirring occasionally. Stir in the noodles.

To serve, ladle the soup into soup bowls and garnish with cilantro.

HATCH PEPPER

SALSAS &
CONDIMENTS

Hatch & Cilantro Caesar Dressing

Hatch & Cilantro Caesar Dressing

makes 2½ to 3 cups

½ cup milk

1 bunch cilantro

2 cloves Melissa's Peeled Garlic, chopped

2 tablespoons Worcestershire sauce

1 tablespoon Tabasco® sauce or Tapatio® sauce

Juice of 1 Melissa's Seedless Lemon

1 tablespoon rice vinegar

½ cup grated Parmesan cheese, divided

1 Melissa's Hatch Pepper, peeled, stemmed, seeded, and diced *(see Hatch Pepper Essentials, page 12)*

2 cups mayonnaise

Kosher salt and freshly ground pepper to taste

In a blender, process the milk, cilantro, garlic, Worcestershire sauce, Tabasco® sauce, lemon juice, vinegar, ¼ cup of the Parmesan, and the Hatch Pepper until well blended.

In a mixing bowl, whisk together the mayonnaise, remaining ¼ cup Parmesan, and milk mixture and season with salt and pepper to taste.

Tomatillo & Hatch Pepper Salsa

makes about 3 cups

1¼ pounds (about 10) Melissa's Fresh Tomatillos

½ Melissa's Perfect Sweet Onion, sliced (about ½ cup)

4 cloves Melissa's Peeled Garlic

2 medium Melissa's Hatch Peppers, roasted, peeled, stemmed, and seeded *(see Hatch Pepper Essentials, page 12)*

1 teaspoon coriander

1 teaspoon oregano

½ teaspoon ground cumin

¼ cup water

Preheat the oven to 425°F.

Remove the thin husks from the tomatillos and rinse the tomatillos. Place the tomatillos, onion, and garlic on a baking sheet, place the baking sheet on the center oven rack, and roast the vegetables until moderately charred, about 15 minutes.

After the vegetables have cooled, place them in a blender, add the Hatch Peppers, coriander, oregano, cumin, and water and process until the desired consistency is reached.

Hatch Pepper Pico de Gallo

makes 4 to 6 servings

6 Roma tomatoes, diced

½ Melissa's Perfect Sweet Onion, diced (about ½ cup)

½ teaspoon Melissa's Hatch Pepper Seasoning

½ teaspoon Melissa's Green Hatch Pepper Powder, mild or hot

4 Melissa's Hatch Peppers, roasted, peeled, stemmed, seeded, and finely chopped *(see Hatch Pepper Essentials, page 12)*

¼ bunch fresh cilantro, chopped

8 Melissa's Key Limes, halved, for juicing

Combine the tomatoes, onion, pepper seasoning, pepper powder, chopped Hatch Peppers, and cilantro in a bowl. Squeeze the lime juice over the tomato mixture and mix well.

Blended Hatch Pepper Salsa

makes 6 to 8 servings

8 Roma tomatoes

1 Melissa's Perfect Sweet Onion, peeled and quartered

3 cloves Melissa's Peeled Garlic

2 tablespoons extra-virgin olive oil

2 tablespoons Melissa's Hatch Pepper Seasoning

2 Melissa's Hatch Peppers, roasted, peeled, stemmed, seeded, and chopped *(see Hatch Pepper Essentials, page 12)*

½ bunch fresh cilantro, chopped

1 teaspoon ground cumin

1 lime, halved, for juicing

Preheat the oven to 425°F.

Arrange the tomatoes, onion, and garlic on a baking sheet and drizzle with the olive oil. Sprinkle with the pepper seasoning and rub in gently. Roast until moderately charred, about 15 minutes.

Combine the roasted vegetables, chopped Hatch Peppers, cilantro, and cumin in a blender, squeeze the lime juice into the blender, and process until the desired texture is reached.

Tropical Tangerine Salsa

makes 6 to 8 servings

6 tangerines, 3 sectioned and 3 juiced

½ green bell pepper, finely diced

½ red bell pepper, finely diced

½ yellow bell pepper, finely diced

1 baby pineapple, peeled and finely diced

3 Melissa's Hot Hatch Peppers, roasted, peeled, stemmed, seeded, and finely diced *(see Hatch Pepper Essentials, page 12)*

In a bowl, combine all of the ingredients and mix well. Serve with fish or poultry.

Hatch Salsa Verde

about 2½ to 3 cups

1 pound (about 8) Melissa's Fresh Tomatillos, husks removed

1 medium onion, cut into rings (about 1 cup)

6 green onions

3 Melissa's Hatch Peppers, roasted, peeled, stemmed, and seeded *(see Hatch Pepper Essentials, page 12)*

2 cloves Melissa's Peeled Garlic

2 tablespoons extra-virgin olive oil

Kosher salt and freshly ground pepper to taste

1 bunch cilantro

Juice of 1 lime

Preheat the oven to 400°F.

In a large bowl, combine the tomatillos, onion, green onions, Hatch Peppers, garlic, olive oil, and salt and pepper to taste and toss to mix. Arrange the vegetables on a baking sheet, bake until tender, about 20 minutes, and set aside to cool.

In a blender, combine the cooled vegetables, cilantro, and lime juice and process until smooth. Serve with your favorite chips, tacos, or eggs.

Basil & Hatch Pepper Pesto

makes 1 cup

2 cups packed fresh basil

1 clove Melissa's Peeled Garlic, chopped

¼ cup Melissa's Pine Nuts

1 tablespoon Melissa's Hatch Pepper Powder, mild or hot

½ cup extra-virgin olive oil

½ teaspoon kosher salt

⅓ cup finely shredded Parmesan cheese

Juice of 1 lime

Place the basil, garlic, pine nuts, and pepper powder in a blender and mix on medium speed. Add the olive oil in a slow stream and then the salt, processing constantly. Blend in the Parmesan and lime juice and add additional salt if needed. Serve on ravioli, gnocchi, or pasta of your choice.

Hatch Pepper Sauce

makes about 2½ cups

10 Melissa's Dried Hatch Pepper Pods, stemmed and seeded

3 cups water

1 clove Melissa's Peeled Garlic

1 teaspoon kosher salt

½ teaspoon ground cumin

½ teaspoon dried oregano

In a saucepan, combine the dried Hatch Pepper pods and water and bring to a boil. Boil gently for 5 minutes, turn off the heat, and let stand for 5 minutes. Pour the peppers and water carefully into a blender, add the garlic, salt, cumin, and oregano, and process until smooth. Use the sauce for enchiladas, wet burritos, or other recipes.

Roasted Hatch Pepper Cream Sauce

makes about 2 cups

3 tablespoons unsalted butter

3 Melissa's Hatch Peppers, roasted, peeled, stemmed, seeded, and chopped *(see Hatch Pepper Essentials, page 12)*

2 tablespoons chopped chives

2 cups sour cream

1 pinch kosher salt

Juice of ½ lime

In a saucepan, melt the butter and add the Hatch Peppers. Sauté, stirring frequently, for 3 minutes. Add the chives, sour cream, and salt and simmer, stirring frequently, until heated through, about 5 minutes. Pour carefully into a blender, add the lime juice, and process until smooth.

Hatch Pepper Ketchup

makes 3 to 4 cups

4 Melissa's Dried Hatch Pepper Pods

1 tablespoon extra-virgin olive oil

1 onion, diced (about 1 cup)

1 (28-ounce) can whole tomatoes

½ cup cider vinegar

2 cloves Melissa's Peeled Garlic

3 tablespoons brown sugar

½ teaspoon dry mustard

½ teaspoon kosher salt

1 dash Worcestershire sauce

2 pinches ground allspice

2 pinches ground cloves

2 pinches ground cinnamon

1 pinch ground cumin

In a bowl, combine the dried Hatch Pepper pods and enough hot tap water to cover and let soak, stirring every few minutes, until evenly plumped and pliable, about 15 to 30 minutes; do not over soak. Discard the stems and seeds.

In a saucepan, heat the olive oil over medium heat. Add the onion and cook, stirring occasionally, until caramelized, about 8 to 10 minutes.

In a blender, combine the softened Hatch Peppers, caramelized onion, tomatoes, vinegar, garlic, brown sugar, dry mustard, kosher salt, Worcestershire sauce, allspice, cloves, cinnamon, and cumin and process until smooth. Pour into a saucepan, simmer for 20 minutes, stirring occasionally, and cool. Store in the refrigerator for up to 3 weeks. Serve in place of your usual ketchup for an added kick.

Hatch Pepper Butter

makes about ½ cup

4 Melissa's Hatch Peppers, roasted, peeled, stemmed, seeded, and diced *(see Hatch Pepper Essentials, page 12)*

8 tablespoons (1 stick) unsalted butter, softened

1 clove Melissa's Peeled Garlic, minced

Kosher salt and freshly ground pepper to taste

In a bowl, combine the Hatch Peppers, butter, and garlic and mix well. Season with salt and pepper to taste and mix well. Shape the butter into a log on a piece of plastic wrap, roll it tightly, and chill until firm. Store in the refrigerator for up to 2 weeks.

DESSERTS

The Devil's Favorite Devil's Food Cake

The Devil's Favorite Devil's Food Cake

makes 16 servings

CAKE

Cooking spray and flour, for cake pan

2 cups granulated sugar

1¾ cups all-purpose flour

1¼ teaspoons baking soda

1 teaspoon baking powder

¾ cup baking cocoa

2 teaspoons Melissa's Hatch Pepper Powder, mild or hot

1 teaspoon kosher salt

1 cup whole milk

½ cup grapeseed or canola oil

2 large eggs

2 tablespoons espresso syrup or coffee extract, or 2 teaspoons espresso coffee powder

¾ cup water

BUTTERCREAM

¾ cup (1½ sticks) unsalted butter, softened

5⅓ cups powdered sugar

1 cup baking cocoa

⅔ cup whole milk

1 tablespoon pure vanilla extract

For the cake, preheat the oven to 350°F. Spray a 9 by 13-inch cake pan with cooking spray and dust with flour.

Sift the sugar, 1¾ cup flour, baking soda, baking powder, baking cocoa, pepper powder, and salt into the large bowl of a stand mixer and mix well. Add the milk, oil, eggs, and espresso syrup and beat at low speed for 1 minute and then at medium speed for 2 minutes.

Bring the water to a boil in a saucepan, drizzle the water into the batter, and stir until blended. Pour the batter into the cake pan and bake until a wooden pick inserted near the center comes out clean, about 40 minutes. Cool the cake completely.

For the buttercream, beat the butter until light and creamy in the bowl of a stand mixer. Add the powdered sugar and baking cocoa and mix well. Add the milk and vanilla extract and beat until well mixed and creamy. Once the cake is completely cooled, frost the cake as desired.

Cinnamon Apple & Hatch Pepper Crumb Cake

makes 12 to 14 servings

CAKE TOPPING

2 tablespoons unsalted butter

½ cup dark rum

3 Granny Smith apples, peeled, cored, and sliced

⅓ cup granulated sugar

1 tablespoon Melissa's Hatch Pepper Powder, mild or hot

CRUMB TOPPING

¾ cup all-purpose flour

1 tablespoon Melissa's Hatch Pepper Powder, mild or hot

¼ cup granulated sugar

¼ cup packed brown sugar

1 teaspoon ground cinnamon

½ teaspoon Chinese five-spice powder

1 pinch kosher salt

4 tablespoons (½ stick) unsalted butter, melted

CAKE

Cooking spray, for cake pan

2 Granny Smith apples, peeled, cored, and finely diced

3 tablespoons all-purpose flour, for coating apples, plus 1 cup all-purpose flour

½ teaspoon baking soda

½ teaspoon baking powder

½ teaspoon ground cinnamon

1 pinch kosher salt

6 tablespoons (¾ stick) unsalted butter, softened

½ cup granulated sugar

⅓ cup Greek yogurt

1 large egg plus 1 egg yolk

1½ tablespoons dark rum

1 teaspoon pure vanilla extract

1 tablespoon Melissa's Hatch Pepper Powder, mild or hot

For the cake topping, melt the butter in a sauté pan over medium heat and stir in the rum. Add the apples, sugar, and pepper powder and cook, stirring constantly, until the sugar is dissolved. Cook until the apples are slightly tender, about 5 minutes, and set aside to cool.

For the crumb topping, combine all of the crumb topping ingredients in a bowl and mix well.

For the cake, preheat the oven to 350°F. Spray a 9 by 13-inch cake pan with cooking spray, line with parchment paper, and spray the parchment paper.

In a bowl, toss the apples with a small amount of flour to coat. Sift together
1 cup flour, baking soda, baking powder, cinnamon, and salt onto a large piece
of parchment paper.

In the large bowl of a stand mixer fitted with the paddle attachment, cream
together the butter and sugar until light and fluffy. Add the yogurt, egg, egg
yolk, rum, and vanilla extract and beat until well mixed. Add the pepper
powder to the flour mixture, fold the parchment paper to resemble a taco, and
add the mixture gradually to the batter, mixing constantly just until blended.
Fold in the apples. Pour the batter into the cake pan, add an even layer of the
cake topping, and top with the crumb topping.

Bake the cake until a wooden pick inserted near the center comes out clean,
about 50 to 60 minutes. Cool the cake completely before serving.

Hatch Pepper & Cheddar Apple Pie

makes 8 to 10 servings

CRUST

¾ cup grated sharp cheddar cheese

⅔ cup all-purpose flour

1 teaspoon Melissa's Red Hatch Pepper Powder, mild or hot

1 pinch kosher salt

6 tablespoons (¾ stick) cold unsalted butter, cubed

1 Melissa's Hatch Pepper, roasted, peeled, stemmed, seeded, and chopped *(see Hatch Pepper Essentials, page 12)*

1 egg yolk

1 teaspoon water

FILLING

3 Granny Smith apples, cored, peeled, and sliced

1 Melissa's Hatch Pepper, roasted, peeled, stemmed, seeded, and chopped *(see Hatch Pepper Essentials, page 12)*

Juice of ½ Melissa's Seedless Lemon

8 tablespoons (1 stick) unsalted butter, melted

½ cup granulated sugar

¼ cup packed brown sugar

¼ cup cornstarch

½ teaspoon ground cinnamon

⅛ teaspoon ground Melissa's Whole Nutmeg

For the crust, pulse together the cheddar, flour, pepper powder, and salt in a food processor, add the butter and Hatch Pepper, and pulse until the dough forms a ball. Shape the dough into a disk, wrap in plastic wrap, and refrigerate for 30 minutes or up to 2 days.

Preheat the oven to 425°F.

Roll the dough out into a ¼-inch-thick circle on a lightly floured surface, press into a pie plate, and trim the edge, reserving the extra dough for the lattice. Place a piece of parchment paper over the dough, top with pie weights, rice, or dried beans, and bake until golden brown, about 16 to 18 minutes. Whisk together the egg yolk and water in a small bowl. Remove the pie weights and parchment paper from the crust, brush the entire crust with some of the egg mixture, and bake until set, about 2 to 3 minutes.

For the filling, reduce the oven temperature to 375°F.

In a saucepan, combine all of the filling ingredients, bring to a hard simmer over medium-high heat, and cook, stirring constantly, until thickened, about 3 to 5 minutes. Cool the filling.

To assemble, add the filling to the crust using a slotted spoon.

Roll out the reserved dough into a square on a lightly floured surface, cut into strips, and weave the strips in a lattice pattern on top of the filling. Brush the lattice with the remaining egg mixture. Bake the pie until the lattice is golden brown, about 15 to 20 minutes.

Spiced Chocolate & Banana Cream Pie

makes 8 servings

BASE

¾ cup chopped semisweet chocolate

¼ cup heavy cream

1 tablespoon unsalted butter

2 tablespoons Melissa's Hatch Pepper Powder, mild or hot

1 baked (9-inch) pie crust

FILLING

3 tablespoons cornstarch

1⅓ cups water

1 (14-ounce) can sweetened condensed milk

2 Melissa's Vanilla Beans

3 egg yolks, beaten

2 tablespoons unsalted butter

1 teaspoon pure vanilla extract

2 bananas, sliced

Heavy cream, sweetened and whipped, for topping

Shaved chocolate, for garnish

For the base, combine the chocolate, cream, butter, and pepper powder in a saucepan over low heat and cook, stirring constantly, until the chocolate is melted and the mixture is smooth, about 10 minutes. Pour into the crust, brush over the side of the crust, and set aside to cool until set.

For the filling, dissolve the cornstarch in the water in a heavy saucepan over medium heat. Stir in the condensed milk. Split the vanilla beans lengthwise, scrape the tiny seeds into the condensed milk mixture, and drop in the pods. Stir in the egg yolks and cook over medium heat, stirring constantly and watching carefully, just until the mixture is thickened, about 3 or 4 minutes. Remove from the heat, strain the filling into a bowl, and stir in the butter and vanilla extract.

To assemble, layer half the bananas evenly over the chocolate base, pour half the filling evenly over the bananas, and layer with the remaining bananas. Spread evenly with the remaining filling and chill the pie until set, about 4 hours. Top the pie with whipped cream and garnish with chocolate shavings.

Hatch Pepper Tres Leches Bread Pudding

makes 12 servings

PUDDING

¼ cup sweetened condensed milk

¼ cup evaporated milk

3 Melissa's Hatch Peppers, roasted peeled, stemmed, and seeded
(see Hatch Pepper Essentials, page 12)

¼ cup heavy cream

8 large eggs

½ cup granulated sugar

1 teaspoon ground cinnamon

6 cups cubed day-old French bread

TOPPING

1 cup sweetened condensed milk

1 cup evaporated milk

2 Melissa's Hatch Peppers, roasted peeled, stemmed, and seeded *(see Hatch Pepper Essentials, page 12)*

1 cup heavy cream

In a blender, combine the condensed milk, evaporated milk, and Hatch Peppers and process until smooth. Strain the mixture into a mixing bowl, add the cream, eggs, sugar, and cinnamon, and whisk until well blended.

Spread the bread evenly in a 9 by 13-inch baking dish, pour the milk mixture evenly over the bread, and set aside until the bread is thoroughly soaked, about 10 minutes. Place the baking dish in a larger baking dish, add enough hot water to reach halfway up the side of the smaller dish, and bake the pudding in the hot water bath for 40 to 45 minutes.

For the topping, combine the condensed milk, evaporated milk, and Hatch Peppers in a blender and process until smooth. Strain the mixture into a saucepan to remove any pepper seeds or peeling. Add the cream, bring to a simmer over medium-high heat, and then remove from the heat.

To finish, pour the topping over the warm pudding, let stand to soak for a few minutes, and serve warm.

Hatch Pepper Pecan & Vanilla Bean Ice Cream

makes about 1 quart

2 cups whole milk

1 cup heavy cream

¾ cup granulated sugar, divided

2 Melissa's Vanilla Beans, split lengthwise

8 Melissa's Hatch Peppers, roasted, peeled, stemmed, seeded, and diced, divided *(see Hatch Pepper Essentials, page 12)*

4 egg yolks

½ teaspoon pure vanilla extract

½ (8½-ounce) package Melissa's Red Hatch Pepper Pecans, chopped

In a saucepan over medium heat, combine the milk, cream, ½ cup of the sugar, vanilla beans, and half the Hatch Peppers and cook, stirring constantly, until bubbles begin to surface around the edge of the pan.

In a small bowl, whisk the egg yolks and remaining ¼ cup sugar until smooth and falls from whisk in a ribbon pattern. Pour some of the milk mixture into the egg mixture and mix well. Pour the egg mixture into the milk mixture in the saucepan and cook over low heat until thick enough to coat the back of a spoon. Strain the mixture into a bowl and stir in the vanilla extract. Place in the refrigerator until completely chilled.

Stir the remaining Hatch Peppers and pecans into the chilled milk mixture, pour the mixture into an ice cream freezer, and freeze according to the manufacturer's instructions.

Roasted Hatch Pepper Ice Cream

makes 1 quart

4 Melissa's Hatch Peppers, roasted, peeled, stemmed, and seeded *(see Hatch Pepper Essentials, page 12)*

1 cup whole milk

2 cups heavy cream

½ cup granulated sugar

¼ cup honey

6 egg yolks

2 tablespoons vanilla extract

In a blender, process the Hatch Peppers and milk until smooth. Pour into a saucepan, add the cream, sugar, and honey, and bring to a low boil over medium heat. Reduce the heat to low and simmer, stirring occasionally, for 5 minutes.

In a mixing bowl, combine the egg yolks and vanilla extract and whisk until the mixture is smooth and pale yellow.

Strain the cream mixture into a bowl to remove any pepper seeds or pepper skin and return the mixture to the saucepan. Ladle ¼ cup of the cream mixture into the eggs, add the egg mixture to the cream mixture, and cook over low heat, stirring constantly, until thick enough to coat the back of a spoon. Remove from the heat and cool.

Pour the mixture into an ice cream freezer and freeze according to the manufacturer's instructions.

Hot & Cold Lemon-Lime Sorbet

makes 6 to 8 servings

2 Melissa's Seedless Lemons

2 limes

1 cup water

1 cup granulated sugar

1 Melissa's Dried Hot Hatch Pepper Pod

1 Melissa's Hatch Pepper, roasted, peeled, stemmed, seeded, and chopped *(see Hatch Pepper Essentials, page 12)*

Grate the outer peel of one of the lemons and juice both lemons to yield 6 tablespoons juice. Grate the outer peel of one of the limes and juice both limes to yield 5 tablespoons juice.

In a saucepan over high heat, bring the water, sugar, and dried Hatch Pepper pod to a boil, stirring constantly. Remove from the heat and stir in the roasted Hatch Pepper, along with the lemon and lime zest and juice. Chill until completely cooled and discard the dried pepper.

Pour the mixture into an ice cream freezer and freeze according to the manufacturer's instructions.

Muscato™ Grape & Hatch Pepper Crepes

makes 6 crepes

⅔ cup cream cheese, softened

¾ cup sour cream

⅓ cup powdered sugar

1 cup Melissa's Red, Green and Black Muscato™ Grapes, halved

1 Melissa's Hatch Pepper, roasted, peeled, stemmed, seeded, and minced *(see Hatch Pepper Essentials, page 12)*

6 Melissa's Crepes

Melissa's White Chocolate Flavored Dessert Sauce, for drizzling

Powdered sugar, for dusting

In the large bowl of a stand mixer fitted with the whisk attachment, combine the cream cheese, sour cream, and powdered sugar and beat until smooth. Stir in the grapes and Hatch Pepper.

Spread a sixth of the cream cheese mixture over the bottom third of a crepe and roll to enclose the filling. Repeat the procedure with the remaining cream cheese mixture and crepes.

To plate, drizzle with the white chocolate sauce and dust with powdered sugar.

Grandma Joyce's Crescent Cookies *with* a Twist

makes about 1 dozen

8 ounces (2 sticks) butter, softened

6 tablespoons powdered sugar

1 teaspoon pure vanilla extract

2 cups all-purpose flour

½ cup chopped Melissa's Red Hatch Pepper Pecans

Powdered sugar, for dusting

Melissa's Hatch Pepper Powder, mild or hot, to taste

Preheat the oven to 350°F.

In the large bowl of a stand mixer, combine the butter and 6 tablespoons powdered sugar and mix well. Add the vanilla extract and flour and beat until well mixed. Mix the pecans into the dough.

Shape the dough into 12 crescent-shape cookies and arrange on an ungreased baking sheet. Bake until golden brown, about 15 minutes.

Remove the cookies to a wire rack and cool completely. Lightly dust with powdered sugar and sprinkle with pepper powder to taste.

Hatch Pecan Brownies

makes 16 brownies

6 tablespoons (¾ stick) unsalted butter, softened

¾ cup granulated sugar

5 large eggs, separated

1 pinch Melissa's Hatch Pepper Seasoning

6 ounces dark baking chocolate

½ (8½-ounce) package Melissa's Red Hatch Pepper Pecans, chopped

2 cups Melissa's Hatch Pepper Kettle Corn

Preheat the oven to 350°F. Grease a 9 by 9-inch baking dish.

In the large bowl of a stand mixer, cream the butter and sugar and mix in the egg yolks and then the pepper seasoning.

Melt the chocolate in the top of a double boiler over medium heat and cool slightly so it won't melt the butter. Add to the butter mixture, mix well, and stir in the pecans.

In the small bowl of a stand mixer, beat the egg whites until soft peaks form. Fold into the batter and combine until mixed and creamy. Pour into the prepared baking dish and sprinkle the kettle corn over the top. Bake until a wooden pick inserted near the center comes out clean, about 45 minutes. Cool for 30 minutes, cut into squares, and serve.

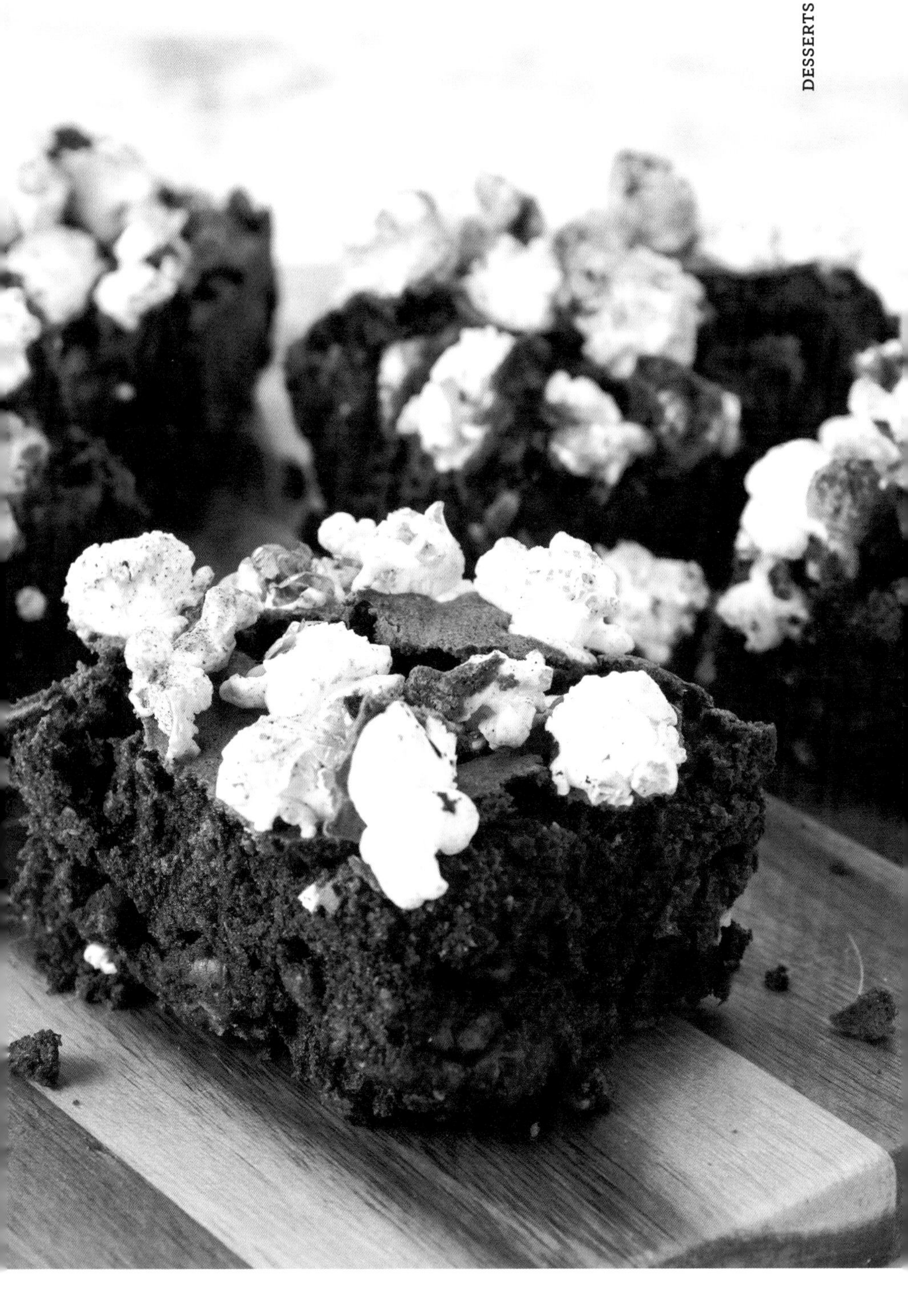

Hatch & Peppermint Bark

makes 6 to 8 servings

12 ounces dark chocolate chips

12 ounces white chocolate chips

12 peppermint candies, crushed

¼ (8½-ounce) package Melissa's Red Hatch Pepper Pecans, chopped

1½ cups Melissa's Hatch Pepper Popcorn

Line a baking sheet with foil.

Place a heatproof bowl over a pot of boiling water, making sure the bottom of the bowl doesn't touch the water. Add the dark chocolate to the bowl, cook, stirring frequently, until melted, and spread evenly in the center of the baking sheet. Chill until the chocolate is hardened.

Melt the white chocolate in a heatproof bowl over a pot of boiling water and remove from the heat. Stir in ¾ each of the peppermints and pecans, and spread evenly over the dark chocolate layer. Sprinkle with the popcorn and remaining peppermints and pecans, pressing lightly into the white chocolate. Chill until the chocolate is completely hardened and then break into pieces.

Chocolate, Caramel, & Pretzel Bark

makes 15 to 20 servings

8 ounces mini pretzels

8 ounces (2 sticks) unsalted butter

1 cup packed brown sugar

1 tablespoon Melissa's Red Hatch Pepper Powder, mild or hot

2 cups dark chocolate chips

1 tablespoon coarse sea salt

½ (5-ounce) package Melissa's Hatch Pepper Kettle Corn

Preheat the oven to 350°F. Line a baking sheet with foil.

Arrange the pretzels in a single layer on the baking sheet and set aside.

Melt the butter in a saucepan over medium heat. Stir in the brown sugar and pepper powder. Pour evenly over the pretzels and bake for 5 minutes. Sprinkle with the chocolate chips and bake for 1 minute. Stir the mixture and spread into a ⅛-inch-thick layer. Sprinkle with the sea salt and kettle corn and press lightly. Cool completely and break into pieces.

Buñuelos *with* Hot Honey Drizzle

makes 4 to 6 servings

Canola oil, for frying

6 (8-inch) flour tortillas

½ cup honey

1 tablespoon Melissa's Hatch Pepper Powder, mild or hot

Powdered sugar, for dusting *(optional)*

In a large skillet, heat ⅛ inch of canola oil over medium-high heat and fry a tortilla, turning once, until golden brown, about 20 to 30 seconds. Drain on paper towels. Repeat the procedure with the remaining tortillas, adding additional canola oil as needed.

In a saucepan, combine the honey and pepper powder, bring to a simmer over medium heat, and remove from the heat. Set aside for 15 minutes to cool slightly.

Arrange the tortillas on a serving platter, drizzle with the hot honey mixture, and dust with powdered sugar.

Hatch Pepper Popcorn Peanut Brittle

makes 15 to 20 servings

Cooking spray

¼ cup water

1 cup granulated sugar

½ cup light corn syrup

2 teaspoons Melissa's Hatch Pepper Seasoning

1 cup salted peanuts

2 tablespoons unsalted butter

1 teaspoon baking soda

½ (5-ounce) package Melissa's Hatch Pepper Kettle Corn

Spray a cookie sheet with cooking spray.

In a saucepan over medium-high heat, bring the water, sugar, corn syrup, and pepper seasoning to a boil and stir until the sugar is dissolved. Stir in the peanuts and cook, stirring frequently, until a candy thermometer inserted in the mixture reads 300°F.

Remove from the heat and immediately stir in the butter and baking soda. Pour the mixture evenly onto the cookie sheet, add the kettle corn, and press lightly. Cool completely and break into pieces.

HATCH PEPPER

DRINKS

Sugar & Spice Cocoa

Sugar & Spice Cocoa

makes 3 to 4 servings

4 cups whole milk

2 Melissa's Dried Hatch Pepper Pods, stems and seeds removed

1 vanilla bean

14 peppermint candies, crushed

½ cup semisweet chocolate chips

Marshmallows, for garnish *(optional)*

Melissa's Chocolate Dessert Sauce, for drizzling *(optional)*

In a saucepan, combine the milk and dried Hatch Pepper pods. Split the vanilla bean lengthwise, scrape the tiny seeds into the milk mixture, and drop the vanilla bean pod into the mixture. Cook over medium-high heat, stirring occasionally, until bubbles begin to surface around the edge of the pan.

Add the crushed peppermints and stir in the chocolate chips. Cook, stirring frequently, until the chocolate is melted, about 5 to 6 minutes. Remove the Hatch Peppers and vanilla bean pod. Garnish with marshmallows and a drizzle of chocolate sauce if desired.

Hatch Pepper Bloody Mary

makes 1 serving

1 cup ice

Melissa's My Grinder® Organic Peppercorns, divided

6 ounces tomato juice

¼ cup Grey Goose® vodka

1 tablespoon A-1® steak sauce

2 teaspoons Worcestershire sauce

2 teaspoons Melissa's Extra Hot Grated Horseradish

1 pinch garlic salt

1 pinch celery salt

Melissa's Hatch Pepper Powder, mild or hot, to taste

1 lime plus 2 wedges, divided

Kosher salt to taste

½ Melissa's Hatch Pepper, roasted, peeled, stemmed, and seeded *(see Hatch Pepper Essentials, page 12)*

1 long thin rib celery

Place the ice in a large cocktail shaker and twist 4 turns of the peppercorn grinder into the shaker. Add the tomato juice, vodka, steak sauce, Worcestershire sauce, horseradish, garlic salt, celery salt, and 1 pinch pepper powder, cover the shaker, and shake vigorously until well blended.

Cut the whole lime into halves and squeeze the juice onto a small plate. On a separate small plate, combine the salt and pepper powder to taste. Dip the rim of a large glass into the lime juice and then into the salt mixture to coat the rim.

Pour the beverage into the glass, squeeze the juice of the lime wedges into the beverage, and drop the wedges into the glass. Wrap the Hatch Pepper onto the celery and place it in the glass. Twist a little more pepper on top and serve.

Hatch, Mango, & Watermelon Margaritas

makes 4 cups purée and 8 cocktails

PURÉE

2 cups chopped watermelon

1 mango, diced

Juice of 2 limes

1 Melissa's Hot Hatch Pepper, roasted, peeled, stemmed, and seeded *(see Hatch Pepper Essentials, page 12)*

1 Melissa's Mild Hatch Pepper, roasted, peeled, stemmed, and seeded *(see Hatch Pepper Essentials, page 12)*

1 cup sugar

1 cup water

COCKTAIL

8 cups ice

2 cups tequila

4 tablespoons granulated sugar

2 tablespoons Melissa's Hatch Pepper Powder, mild or hot

1 lime, cut into 8 wedges

For the purée, combine all of the purée ingredients in a blender and process until smooth. The purée may be stored in the refrigerator for up to 1 week.

For the cocktail, combine the purée, ice, and tequila in a blender and process until smooth or serve the purée and tequila over the ice.

On a small plate, combine the sugar and pepper powder. Moisten the rim of each glass with a lime wedge and then dip the rim into the sugar mixture to coat the rim. Pour the beverage into the glasses and garnish each with a lime wedge.

Banana, Mango, & Hatch Pepper Agua Fresca

makes 3 or 4 servings

1 mango, peeled, halved, and pitted

1 banana

1 Melissa's Hatch Pepper, roasted, peeled, stemmed, and seeded
(see Hatch Pepper Essentials, page 12)

2 cups water

1 cup milk

¼ cup granulated sugar

Combine all of the ingredients in a blender, process until smooth, and serve cold.

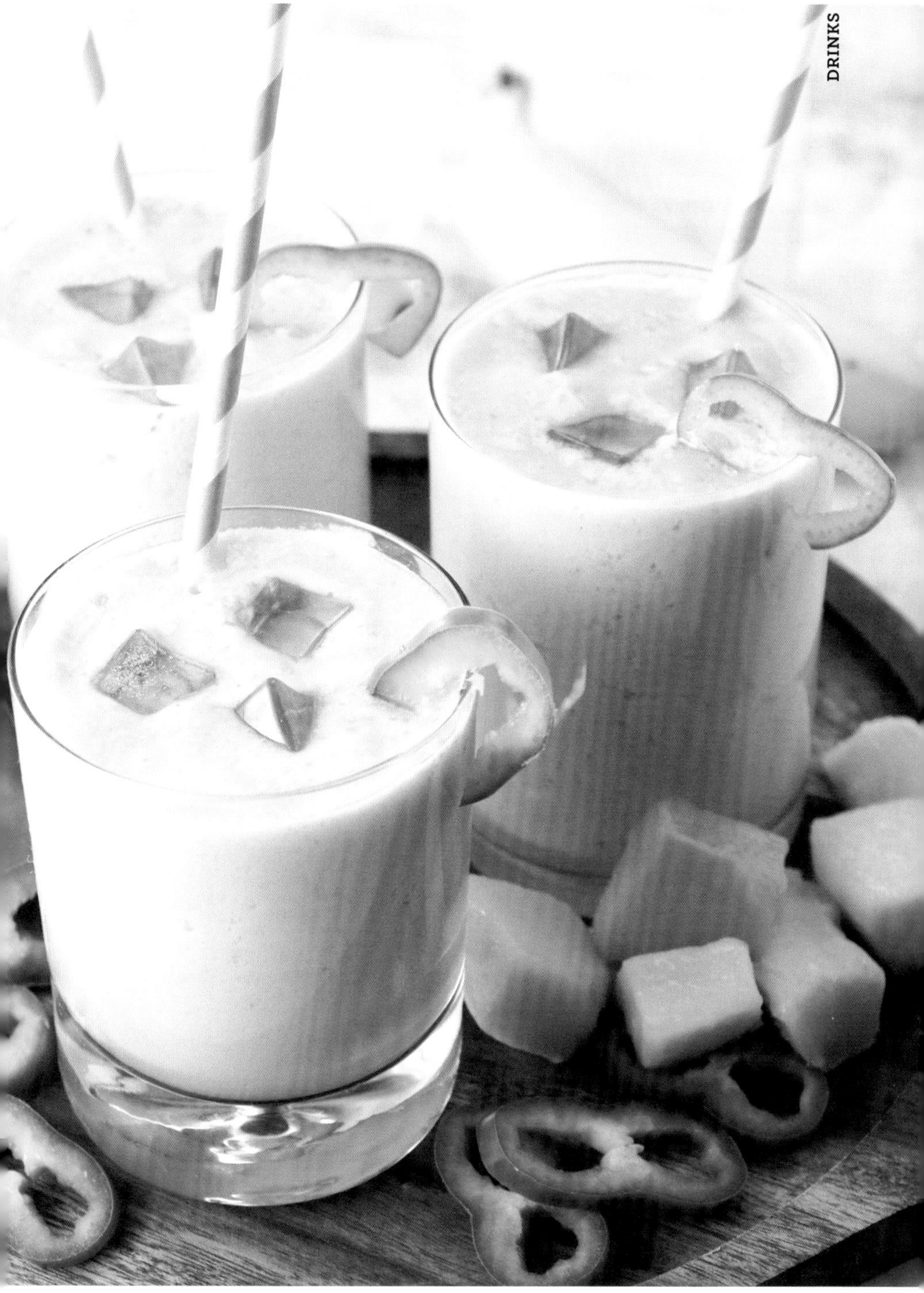

Hatch Pepper & Berry Agua Fresca

makes 8 to 10 servings

½ cup water

½ cup granulated sugar

2 tablespoons Melissa's Hatch Pepper Powder, mild or hot

1 pound (about 16) fresh strawberries, hulled

12 ounces fresh blueberries

5 cups cold water

In a saucepan, combine ½ cup water, sugar, and pepper powder and bring to a simmer, stirring to dissolve the sugar. Chill in the refrigerator for up to 3 days.

In a blender, combine the strawberries, blueberries, and 5 cups cold water and process until well mixed. Blend in the desired amount of the sugar mixture and serve in chilled glasses.

Hatch, Mango, & Berry Smoothie

makes 2 servings

1 Melissa's Hatch Pepper, roasted, peeled, stemmed, and seeded
(see Hatch Pepper Essentials, page 12)

1 Melissa's Sapūrana Mango, peeled, seeded, cubed, and frozen

½ cup frozen raspberries

½ banana, frozen

½ cup vanilla yogurt

½ cup cold whole milk

1 pinch ground cayenne pepper

In a blender, combine all of the ingredients and process until smooth. Pour into 2 chilled glasses and serve.

Index